# The Uncommon Gospel

*GRACE THAT RUINS RELIGION*

Jess Hays

The Uncommon Gospel: Grace That Ruins Religion

Copyright © 2025 by Jess Hays
All rights reserved.

ISBN: 979-8268010909


All Scripture quotations, unless otherwise indicated, are taken from the New English Translation (NET).


All rights reserved. No part of this publication may be reproduced, stored in a retrieval system, or transmitted in any form by any means—electronic, mechanical, photocopy, recording, or any other—except for brief quotations in printed reviews, without the permission of the author.


Website: renegadegrace.com
Email: jess@renegadegrace.com
Instagram: @renegadepastor

# Table of Contents

Enter at Your Own Risk ..................................................... 9
Radical Favor ..................................................................... 15
Finished Forgiveness ....................................................... 31
New Life ............................................................................ 51
Complete Closeness ......................................................... 63
Holy Nature ...................................................................... 79
Total Dependence ............................................................ 95
Fresh Fruit ........................................................................ 117
Final Thoughts ................................................................. 135
Verse References ............................................................. 139

*For the church.*

*May you awaken to the truth of a radical, unconditional, and life changing gospel.*

"If you've ever suspected that God is way better than the rule-keepers advertised, *The Uncommon Gospel* will feel like a spiritual jailbreak. Jess Hays takes religion's sacred cows, seasons them with Paul's spiciest epistles, and serves them medium-rare. Her message is unapologetically disruptive: Grace isn't a reward for good behavior but erupts from the unstoppable character of God Himself. Expect to be comforted, offended, relieved, and provoked—sometimes all in the same paragraph. Read this book if you're brave enough to trade spiritual anxiety for real freedom in Jesus."

**Andrew Farley**
**Bestselling author of *The Naked Gospel***
**Nationally syndicated radio host of *The Grace Message***
**Founder of BibleQuestions.com**

# Enter at Your Own Risk

I spent a good chunk of my life believing I knew God and what He was about. My formative years were spent in training under the watchful eye of a religion which taught me that God's love was waiting on me. It was waiting for me to ask for forgiveness, waiting for me to draw near, waiting for me to stop sinning, waiting for me to study more, waiting for me to be more committed. Waiting on me. Oh, sure, He loved me and wanted to have a relationship with me, but we couldn't really be close until I was more like Him. Oh, and being like Him was progressive, slow, and required great effort on my part. The Bible was "very clear" about this, religion said.

That's a favorite phrase of religious people, "the Bible is very clear," after which comes a spouting of some form of doctrine that they have carefully interpreted scripture to fit within. Who was I to question anything that the Bible was "very clear" about? I did question, though, often and with great fervor, much to the chagrin of the church. It has been my experience that legalistic people find questions to be very frustrating.

The legalists in my life found a workaround, though. They pointed me in the direction of education. "Here, just study this lesson series, read this pastor's book, go to apologetics camp and learn to defend your faith!" Don't get me wrong, they didn't have to twist my arm or anything. I've always been just a little too much of a learner. Unfortunately, in spite of my education, persistent study, and intelligence, everything that the church taught me about the gospel seemed contradictory and I was still not able to find the answers to my questions.

Until I did. And it ruined everything I thought I knew about God and about me.

It was the book of Romans that ultimately did it for me, Paul's letter that is dripping with the doctrine of grace. Growing up, I had not ever really heard much about grace, at least not in any real, deep, or meaningful way. Grace was just about getting saved. After that, there wasn't much to talk about. I had just finished reading a book, *The Naked Gospel*, that spoke about grace in a very different way, a radical and life-altering way. And it messed me up a little bit. I was sure that the immense grace the author wrote about couldn't possibly be true, and if it was, why hadn't I learned about it in church? Into Romans I went, sure that I would find the Bible to be *very clear* on the subject.

And clear it was.

Clear that grace is a free gift. (Romans 3:24; 5:15)

Clear that grace is radical. (Romans 5:20-21)

Clear that grace gives us power over sin. (Romans 6:14)

Clear that grace needs nothing, expects nothing, and gives everything. (Romans 8:32)

Clear that forgiveness is finished. (Romans 6:10)

Clear that closeness with God is not conditional. (Romans 8:38-39)

Clear that faith is about receiving from God, not doing more for Him. (Romans 4:5)

Clear that God is for me. (Romans 8:31)

Clear that I am filled with goodness. (Romans 15:14)


It was VERY clear.


And I became obsessed with finding out everything I could about this kind of grace.


Suddenly, every verse I thought I knew that seemed to call me to more effort was ruined by eyes of grace that now saw God's goodness as the source and not the prize at the end. Suddenly, every Christian book I read, worship song I sang, and sermon I heard became frustrating as I became aware of just how deep Satan has his claws in Christianity and the church.

Do you know how many well-educated, seminary-degree-possessing Christians with "Dr." at the front of their name don't understand the bigness of grace? Too many. Most Christian churches talk about grace to some degree, but rarely do they remove religion's filter, instead sifting grace through added religious commitment so it doesn't become "too dangerous." Hundreds of pastors stand behind pulpits every Sunday and preach a message soaked in self-effort and transactional relationship while the apostles' letters urge us to believe the opposite. Despite the almost two thousand years that have passed, it seems that we are no better off than those foolish Galatians!

---

*"You foolish Galatians! Who has cast a spell on you? Before your eyes Jesus Christ was vividly portrayed as crucified. The only thing I want to learn from you is this: Did you receive the Spirit by doing the works of the law or by believing what you heard? Are you so foolish?* **Although you began with the Spirit, are you now trying to finish by human effort**" *(Galatians 3:1-3)*

---

So, I am writing this book for every Christian who has ever been taught a gospel that gets worse after you get saved and for the ones who have been told to do better, try harder, work for the blessing, and die daily. This book is for the church. This is for my brothers and sisters who continue to live embedded in a fractured gospel that offers a hard yoke and a heavy burden. My heart aches for you to know the good news of Jesus that is easy and light.

Though it should be, the radical message of the gospel is not common knowledge in the church, which is why this book exists. It contains in it a gospel that sounds too good to be true but is. If you dare to believe it, you will find that it is both ruin and restoration. It will simultaneously ruin your best efforts at perfection and restore your greatest failures. It is both demolition of religion and construction of faith. That might be the most beautiful thing about the true gospel, that it is both wreckage and renewal and we are left with no other choice but to be overcome with its goodness or settle for driftwood.

Once you know the truth about how good God's grace really is, it will ruin you for anything else.

Consider this your warning shot.

# Radical Favor

RUINING THE RELIGION OF A WITHHOLDING GOD

I grew up entrenched in religion. We were a family of religion with a lineage of religion, ministers in every generation. It would not surprise me if my mother were to tell me that my first words were a Bible verse, or at the very least, a few hummed hymn bars. If Paul was a "Jew of Jews," then we were the "Baptists of Baptists." Well… at least as far as anyone could tell.

In spite of the excessive amount of "Christian education" I received throughout my childhood, I don't remember hearing about grace very often. When I did, it was only ever in reference to my salvation, "by grace through faith" we'd repeat like a mantra. My understanding of grace for most of my life was only as a concept, an action, something that God did or something that God gave. This is not untrue about grace, but it is only one small piece of grace. In this limited understanding, grace then became only for heaven some day and had little impact on my every day.

Since that time, I have heard no shortage of talk about grace and have been offered many definitions of it. Still, it seems the church is convinced that grace is simply God's response to sin thus connecting sin and grace together. This is evidenced by our most common definition of grace that always comes in a combo pack with mercy.

We define mercy as "not getting what we deserve" which *is* directly related to sin and not receiving our just punishment for it. This is a good and accurate definition of mercy. The problem comes when we treat mercy and grace as a BOGO deal—defining grace as "getting what we don't deserve," or simply "unmerited favor." While not untrue, these tie grace too closely to mercy, and by extension, to sin. We naturally conclude, therefore, that grace is connected to our sin.

By defining grace as "unmerited favor," we are introducing the idea that in some way our merit impacts God's favor. So then, the prerequisite for grace is that we must have failed to earn it. This makes grace a result of or God's response to our sin rather than what it really is, which is the core nature of God's character. Yes, grace is unearnable, but that is because grace is not transactional. Whether we do or do not have merit is not part of the calculation at all. It's about God's character, not ours.

Grace is the limitless, one-way, no-strings-attached love and favor of God. Simply put, it is God's *unconditional* favor. Grace is God's goodness actively at work on our behalf. Grace is the identity of God that pursues us with the purpose of loving us. Grace is the language of God's heart that speaks to the depths of our being. The bigness of God's grace is not only in His forgiveness of our every fault and failure, but also in the intertwining of His life within us, freeing the places we forgot were held captive.

The Greek word for grace found throughout New Testament scripture is **charis** which means "favor, disposed to, inclined, favorable towards, leaning towards to share benefit."[1] I especially like the last part of that definition, "leaning towards to share benefit." Isn't that an interesting way to define grace? Grace then becomes God's action of always leaning towards us. And for what reason is He leaning towards us? To deal with our sin? No, *to share benefit*. What benefit exactly? The benefit of *Him*.

I have spent the last 15 years of my life obsessing over grace, studying grace, and asking the Lord to reveal the truth about grace to me. In that time, I have now come to understand that, in reality, grace is God's expression of His identity. Bill Thrall said once on his podcast *Living Influence,* "Grace is how the Trinity treats one another."[2] Bill cites John's description of Jesus being "full of grace and truth" commenting, "Jesus came to earth and brought grace with Him. He didn't pick it up on His way here! It was the only realm in which He ever lived." Wow. Now that's something radical to consider. Grace is the culture of heaven, how God relates to Himself.

---

> *"And the Word became flesh, and dwelt among us; and we saw his glory, glory as of the only Son from the Father, **full of grace and truth**. John testified about him and called out, saying, "This was he of*

---

[1] James Strong, The New Strong's Exhaustive Concordance of the Bible, Nashville: T. Nelson, 1990, s.v. " charis"
[2] Bill Thrall, "Grace Began Within the Trinity," Living Influence, Ep.16

> whom I said, 'he who is coming after me has proved to be my superior, because he existed before me.'"
> **For of his fullness we have all received, and grace upon grace.** For the Law was given through Moses; **grace and truth were realized through Jesus Christ**." *(John 1:14-17 NASB)*

---

Grace is God's pouring out who He is onto us. Sin is not a factor. If this were an Excel spreadsheet, sin would give us a #REF error in our grace equation (that joke's just for me). God will continue to be God regardless of how we behave, and so grace will continue to be grace. That is what **unconditional** means.

*So, what are you saying? That everyone just gets grace no matter what?*

I mean, pretty much, yeah. Even unbelievers experience some form of grace, a taste of grace, just simply in the fact that they are alive and breathing and still have the opportunity to accept Christ. If God were not being gracious, then He would just come now, zap up all the Christians, and go about His merry way. One of my favorite verses that highlights this is 2 Peter 3:9, **"The Lord is not slow concerning his promise, as some regard slowness, but is being patient toward you, because he does not wish for any to perish but for all to come to repentance."** God's grace for unbelievers is seen in His patience towards them and His desire that they would believe. Scripture tells us that it is His kindness that draws unbelievers to Him (Romans 2:4). He is permanently leaning in.

While everyone experiences a taste of grace, the fullness of God's grace can only be experienced through oneness with Him. The access point for this oneness is faith in Christ.

> *"For by grace you are saved **through faith**, and this is not from yourselves, it is the gift of God; it is not from works, so that no one can boast."*
> *(Ephesians 2:8-9)*

I recognize that most of you reading this are already believers and so you already have oneness in Christ. You already have the fullness of grace in you. What part does faith have to play for you?

For the unbeliever, faith creates *access* to oneness. For the believer, faith creates *awareness* of oneness. Before I get into that, it's important that we understand faith.

What is faith exactly?

Many scholars have argued over it, many pastors call for us to have it, even the world in its depravity demands it of us, though it calls it by a different name. Every day we walk through life having faith and lacking it without ever stopping to think about it.

We have faith that the government is going to protect us from invasion.

We have faith that the seat belts in our cars will keep us safe.

We have faith that our friends won't betray our secrets.

We have faith that the extra shot of espresso will overcome our lack of sleep. (Is that just me or...?)

Every religion has something to say about faith. Whether it be your need for it, your lack of it, the power of it, or the promise of it, the one thing most religions are in agreement on is that with deity, faith is a requirement. Again, we have made faith simply about accessing salvation.

One of the most significant things to me about God is that He loves us enough to give us a choice. For as long as I can remember, I have despised the idea of being controlled. When I was a child, this presented itself by my constant questioning, propensity to push boundaries, significant outbursts of anger when I didn't get my way, and just my general knack for finding trouble. A lot of adults spent a lot of time trying to force me to fit in boxes, and I obviously had a cardboard allergy. I didn't *mean* to be this way. I just was. I didn't intentionally challenge everyone and everything, I was just naturally that way. I was born for freedom and also born into fundamentalism, which, as it turns out, are mutually exclusive. So, for me, Jess the challenger, one of the kindest things God ever did was give me a choice.

However enticing and amazing God's grace may be, it is not irresistible. God's love is not abusive. It is not unkind. It does not demand. God will pursue you. He will never give up on you, *and* He will not force Himself on you. God gives His grace freely as a gift, and you must choose whether or not to receive it.

Faith is simply a choice to receive what God freely gives. Faith is an intentional entering into dependence and reliance on Christ.

Because of this, faith does not retire after our one trusting of God for salvation but continues into our lived-out Christian life. This is why faith, for the believer, creates *awareness* of oneness. Faith allows us to get rid of old thinking and belief patterns and accept the truth of who God is and how He relates to us. This awareness will lead to growth and good behavior, but that good behavior is still rooted in faith and not effort.

> *"And God is able to make **all grace** overflow to you so that because you have enough of everything in every way at all times, you will **overflow** in every good work." (2 Corinthians 9:8)*

Yes, grace is for salvation, and, also, it's for daily life.

Yes, grace is God's action towards sin, and, also, it's His nature of favor.

Yes, grace is for heaven, and, also, it's now.


The church has neglected the fullness of grace because we do not understand it. We have set it aside, either in the past with our conversion or in the future with our eternity. As a result, for our present, we have elected instead for the way of this world, measuring goodness with good effort and perceived morality. Instead of finding our identity in Christ, we have chosen to find it in our behavior. "I am what I do," we unintentionally say.


Grace is difficult for us to fully understand because it's native to heaven's culture and not to ours. It's difficult for us to imagine the possibility of receiving something as remarkable as God's full favor.  See, that's why faith is the only requirement, because grace calls us to believe in something that is the opposite of human culture.  It requires no effort from us while giving us everything we could never earn.  That was the whole point of Jesus.  A Deity full of grace and truth, who stepped into the brittleness of humanity, walked with dusty feet among dirty people, and died so that the men who killed Him could have righteousness.  It takes faith to believe in that kind of love, an extreme form of affection that came from a God that we forsook.  That is the radical favor that God is eager for you to know.

But you still have a choice.

You can choose to work by the system of this world if you want.  It's a system that measures your goodness based on how well you do this or that, how perfectly you behave, and how many failures you avoid.  You can try your best, exert your greatest effort, and try to earn that spiritual paycheck, but that sounds pretty exhausting, doesn't it? Not only that, but all that energy and all that work is worthless compared to Christ.  In fact, the prophet Isaiah goes as far as to say that **"our so-called righteous acts are like a menstrual rag in God's sight." (Isaiah 64:6)**

You have another option.  You can choose to believe in the gift of grace.  You can trust the fullness of Christ's action on your behalf.  It is a grace that keeps and satisfies all expectations, a grace that doesn't just overlook our failures but actually redefines us as successes, a grace from which you can never be disqualified.  You have it already.  It's yours, just waiting for you to choose to believe.

I know it's hard to believe. It feels too good to be true. The first time I ever heard about this kind of grace, I thought so, too. As I mentioned briefly earlier, my first encounter with radical grace theology came through a book, *The Naked Gospel,* by Andrew Farley. I don't even remember who gave me the book -- I think maybe my therapist -- but somehow it ended up in my apartment. I read the book, and I had two immediate reactions.

1) This makes every question I've ever had about my faith make sense.
2) This is *way* too good to be true.

Me, being me, I decided to try and prove him wrong. I was very compelled by how much scripture he used in that book, but that also meant that in order to effectively prove him wrong I had to do it with scripture. Unfortunately for me, I decided to start by reading the book of Romans. Pro Tip: If you want to disprove extreme grace, don't read the book of Romans. Instead, I found myself even deeper down the rabbit hole of radical grace, and for the first time ever in my life, I was really *happy* to be wrong about something.

Up to that point in my life as a Christian, for as long as I could remember, I had been both enamored with Jesus and disgusted with myself. Maybe they were connected? Because I was disgusted with myself, I became enamored with this Jesus I read about who had a propensity for embracing disgusting people. This dichotomy created an inner war in me of *feeling* unlovable and also *knowing* that Jesus loved me. These were two things that I couldn't reconcile. Religion was more than happy to offer me a solution to this puzzle in the form of God "the Father" who served as the hardened judge to deal with my disgustingness. So, I adopted a theology that was, "Jesus loves me. God tolerates me (sort of, but only if I hide behind Jesus)."

This is not a unique theology. In fact, it might be the most common theology in the church today. Of course, they rarely say it as directly as I've said here. Instead, it sounds more like, "When God looks at you, He sees Jesus and not your sin. You're a sinner who is just covered under the blood. Jesus is in heaven acting as your divine defense attorney with the Father."

So... God and Jesus aren't in agreement about me? A house divided? They're having an eternal family argument about me?

Looking back, this theology seems silly and illogical to me. It requires a belief in ongoing disunity within the Trinity and, as I hope to demonstrate throughout this book, certainly doesn't align with the whole of scripture. I fell for the age-old human trap of letting what I felt to be true about *me* determine what I believed to be true about *God*. I felt bad, broken, and distant and so I believed that God saw me that way. I happily cherry-picked verses to fortify my feelings.

In our humanness, it's easy for us to get caught up in our feelings. In many ways, our feelings are how we experience the world around us and so, often, we mistakenly allow them to sit in the driver's seat.

So then, we find ourselves going through seasons where God *feels* very detached and very distant. We *feel* disconnected and alone. We *feel* dirty and discarded. The truth is though we may, for whatever reason, *feel* separate from God, He is constantly intertwined in us. He is close. He is jumping up and down and flailing His arms right in front of us while we look around wondering, "God, where are you?!"

As someone who lives with depression, I can honestly tell you that feelings cannot be trusted. They will lie to you to get their way. They will trick you into believing you're the only one who has them and no one could possibly understand. So, if you feel alone and distant, listen to the words of Paul from that pesky book of Romans:

> *For I am convinced that neither death, nor life, nor angels, nor heavenly rulers, nor things that are present, nor things to come, nor powers, nor height, nor depth,* **nor anything else in creation will be able to separate us from the love of God in Christ Jesus our Lord.** *(Romans 8:38-39)*

We are radically loved and completely close to God. There is nothing that can change that. Nothing can separate us from His love. Don't let your feelings lie to you!

Now, I'm not saying that our feelings are evil or invalid. Emotions are a part of being human. They have a purpose and a design. Emotions are great responders, but they are not good leaders. Emotions serve kind of like a motion sensor alarm. If we experience pain, pleasure, frustration, or failure in our lives, our emotions alert us of their presence. We have to be careful though because sometimes we get false alarms.

I work in corporate America and go into an office every day. I get to work a little before 6:00 a.m. every day, and so I am typically the first one in the office and have the whole place to myself for at least an hour before the next person shows up. One early, stormy morning I was sitting at my desk, sipping on my coffee, listening to the rain, and working on a spreadsheet when I heard the front door motion sensor go off. My fight or flight immediately kicked in, and I reached into my bag for the taser I carried with me. (Listen, this is Texas. You're lucky it wasn't something else in my bag.) Taser in hand, I cautiously made my way towards the front door with my back to the wall, because I watch too many procedural cop shows. The motion sensor went off again. *That's weird?* When I arrived at the door, I found the culprit. The wind was so strong from our lovely Texas thunderstorm that it was pushing the door open just enough to trigger the motion sensor. Since the wind was untaseable, I opted instead for pushing a box up against the door to keep it from moving.

In the same way that a motion sensor can't identify if an intruder is an actual real person or just the wind, so our emotions cannot determine to this detail either. They are just an alarm going off. Sometimes they tell us we are in danger, or we should be afraid, but really, it's just the wind of our humanity blowing through our souls. Our feelings don't define reality. They are real, but they are not reality.

As humans, pain is a very real part of our lives. It weaves its way into our memories, hides in the shadows of our addictions, and hunkers down in the corners of our failures. It's so tangible, so visible, so very real that, at times, it becomes hard for us to see anything outside of it.

Pain hollows out these nooks in our scars that bitterness makes a home in. It gouges valleys in our souls where regret and feelings of failure build cities fortified by the words of the broken people who bump into us. And we feel helpless, broken, and without hope.

It's hard to remember the truth about our relationship with God in those moments. It's hard because pain has convinced us that we are not good enough for Him, that we are too broken for Him to want, that who we are can't possibly be loved by someone as glorious as Him. Worse still, pain may have even convinced us that Jesus couldn't possibly understand our pain. Our pain taunts us with whispers of, "He's perfect and you're not; He never hurt the way you hurt." And we believe the whispers because it makes so much sense to us who have been taught of a God who is distant from us. But the truth is, He is Emmanuel, God *with* us.

So often we focus so intently on the power of His deity, His touching death and bringing life, His commanding of storms to silence, and His glory in resurrection that we miss His humanity. We miss His loud sobs at losing a friend. We miss His anxious, bloody drops of sweat as He pleaded for rescue from His purpose. We miss His tender care for desperate people looking for some kind of relief from the same pain that haunts us. The happiest of ever-afters came at the end of the story that began with "Jesus wept," that God would be near to us even on the nights when He *feels* painfully distant. We can take comfort in knowing that the most beautiful of endings come after tears.

So great a God we serve that not only did He speak us into existence with one breath, but also, He slipped into skin and walked among us. Who Jesus was in His humanity is God's tangible picture of who He is and how He relates to us. Jesus is God the Father in human form. They are unified in Their opinion of you. Our God is not a stranger to the sting of pain, not even to the sting of our pain. We hurt, and He is there with us, because through grace, we have oneness.

It's okay to hurt, to cry excessive, overdramatic sobs. It's okay to be heartbroken and fall apart in the midst of the darkness that pain brings with it, but don't let pain make cities. Don't let it define you. Don't let it convince you that God doesn't understand you, doesn't want you, or is not close to you. Don't let it drive you to hopelessness.

Our hurt and hardships don't magically go away when we become a Christian. Knowing the depth of God's radical favor won't keep you from pain or promise you a comfortable life, nor does the existence of pain indicate that you are without His favor. The promise is not for an easy, comfortable life. The promise is that He is with us in it.

---

*"The Lord is near the brokenhearted; he delivers those who are discouraged." (Psalm 34:18)*

*"I have told you these things so that in me you may have peace. In the world you have trouble and suffering but take courage—I have conquered the world." (John 16:33)*

*Blessed is the God and Father of our Lord Jesus Christ, the Father of mercies and God of all comfort, who comforts us in all our troubles so that we may be able to comfort those experiencing*

> *any trouble with the comfort with which we
> ourselves are comforted by God."*
> *(2 Corinthians 1:3-4)*

---

You are held by One who understands your pain. You are comforted by One who relates to your struggle. You are cradled on a chest scarred by the hatred of this world. You are loved more than you could possibly imagine.

Take heart, my friends, in knowing that even when you feel as if you are not enough for Him, He will always be enough for you. Rest in the knowledge that even when you feel dissatisfied in Him, He is satisfied with you. There is nothing more for you to do but lean back and relax in the truth of His radical favor for you.

The intensity of this favor is demonstrated not, as I once thought, in His loving us despite our disgustingness, but rather in the fact that He went to the cross to remove the most disgusting things about us. The Father, then, is not tolerating us as we cower behind Christ. He loves us, delights in us, and is proud to call us His kids because the cross actually worked and we've actually been fully forgiven.

# Finished Forgiveness

RUINING THE RELIGION OF BEGGING FOR FORGIVENESS

Growing up, I was kind of a weird kid. I didn't think so at the time. Things I thought, felt, and were passionate about seemed normal to me, but hindsight is 20/20 as they say. I was hard-headed, passionate, and a little too smart for my own good. Truth, justice, and fairness mattered to me. My brain has always been very black and white in its thinking, and so everything I cared about was at a level 10 in terms of how much it mattered (I'm not sure I ever grew out of that). My natural personality and general inability to filter myself got me in plenty of trouble with both my peers and my authority figures. I learned quickly that, on the playground of life, when you're a kid who's different from other kids, you basically have two choices: you get tough or you get crushed. I got tough. Really tough. Possibly too tough?

People learned quickly not to mess with me. When people did mess with me, well, my skill with my fists was one thing, but more so was my ability to crush people with my words. Somehow, I knew how to sniff out their most sensitive vulnerabilities and then, you know, poke them. I could remember every bad thing they had ever said or done to me, and I would skillfully pull them out when I needed to and unleash it like a weapon.

One day, my dad had a conversation with me about this. I don't remember exactly, but I'm sure he took me to McDonald's or somewhere to lull me into a false sense of security with ice cream and french fries. Pitbulls tend to be nicer to you when you give them food.

"You have to stop bringing up the past when you're arguing with people," he told me in his best concerned, calm dad tone.

"Why?!" I questioned, heatedly. He sighed and shook his head smiling. "Why" was always my favorite question to ask. (Maybe it still is?)

"Because," he answered, "that's fighting dirty."

*Fighting dirty?! I don't fight dirty! If I'm going to beat someone, it will be fair and square!*

"Hmmf," I grumbled in response.

God doesn't fight dirty. He doesn't fight with us at all, actually. Instead, He says, **"Their sins and their lawless deeds I will remember no longer."** (Hebrews 10:17) The next verse continues to tell us **"Now where there is forgiveness of these, there is no longer any offering for sin."** God has fought our sin and won (fair and square). He has no beef with us, and He will never bring up our sin to us because He doesn't even remember it. The one and only confession He wants from us is the confession of that truth.

I have yet to meet any Christian who wouldn't agree that Jesus forgave our sins. That's basically the one core belief on which all Christians can agree. Baptism, communion, which version of the Bible is best, and speaking in tongues there's a flurry of differing ideas about, but Jesus having died to forgive us, that one we're all sure about. Right?

Well, sure, we agree that Jesus forgave our sins, but exactly how many of our sins did He forgive? I grew up hearing a gospel that sounded like this: When you're saved, all your past sins are forgiven, but from then on, you need to ask for forgiveness every time you sin. So then, essentially the gospel gets worse after you're a Christian. My problem with this narrative is simple, God said **all**, like, repeatedly.

> "And even though you were dead in your transgressions and in the uncircumcision of your flesh, he nevertheless made you alive with him, having forgiven **all** your transgressions."
> (Colossians 2:13)

> "By his will we have been made holy through the offering of the body of Jesus Christ **once for all**. And every priest stands day after day serving and offering the same sacrifices again and again—sacrifices that can never take away sins. But when this priest had offered **one sacrifice for sins for all time**, he sat down at the right hand of God."
> (Hebrews 10:10-12)

> *"For the death he died, he died to sin **once for all**, but the life he lives, he lives to God." (Romans 6:10)*

---

All means all.  That means past sins, present sins, and future sins.  Why?  Because unless you are a time traveling professor in a DeLorean, you weren't around when Jesus died, so all of your sins were in the future.  Therefore, in order for *any* of our sins to be forgiven, then *all* of them must be.  Even if you reject a linear timeline with regards to forgiveness, all still means all. Nowhere in scripture are we taught of a parceled-out forgiveness for our sins.  The price for this fullness of forgiveness is blood because the cost of sin is death (Romans 6:23).  This has always been true of forgiveness as shadowed by the Old Covenant sacrifices.

Back in the Old Testament, under the covenant of the Law, to escape punishment, obtain forgiveness, and receive a measure of peace with God, a person brought and offered specific sacrifices to God.  Then, once a year, the high priest would offer one sacrifice for the entire nation of Israel.  This was called the Day of Atonement.   In Hebrew, "to atone" means "to cover" or "to appease."  The Day of Atonement was a day of sin covering, through blood, to appease the just requirement of covenant breaking (death).

The Day of Atonement (Leviticus 16) had very specific rules and regulations and was only to be completed by the high priest.  If the high priest disobeyed any of these rules, he would be immediately struck dead upon entering into the Holy of Holies to make the sacrifice before God.  All this sounds pretty intense and heavy, doesn't it? Yet, again, we see that forgiveness is not something man can gain on His own.  Even in the depth of the Law, we still see that forgiveness of sins was dependent upon *God* receiving the high priest's sacrifice. For those of us who live after the cross, under a New Covenant, we experience Jesus as both our high priest and our sacrificial lamb.

Check out these verses from Hebrews 9:23-26:

***²³ So it was necessary for the sketches of the things in heaven to be purified with these sacrifices, but the heavenly things themselves required better sacrifices than these.***

The sacrifices of the Law were only a picture, a sketch, of what was really required and necessary to satisfy the requirements—a picture pointing to a bigger reality. However, these sacrifices did not fully satisfy God's requirement for dealing with sin. (See also Hebrews 10:1)

***²⁴ For Christ did not enter a sanctuary made with hands—the representation of the true sanctuary—but into heaven itself, and he appears now in God's presence for us.²⁵ And he did not enter to offer himself again and again, the way the high priest enters the sanctuary year after year with blood that is not his own, ²⁶ᵃ for then he would have had to suffer again and again since the foundation of the world.***

Christ is the better sacrifice. He is the bigger reality that the Day of Atonement was shadowing, and His sacrifice was perfect, sufficient, and complete. The high priests of old had to keep coming every year because their sacrifice was never as perfect as Christ's would be. Jesus is not up in heaven dying over and over again. Once was enough to deal with sin entirely.

***²⁶ᵇ But now he has appeared <u>once for all</u> at the consummation of the ages to <u>put away sin</u> by his sacrifice.***

Jesus offers a better sacrifice that is once for all time. The phrase "put away" also translated "take away" here is important. The

Greek is **athetésis** which means "cancellation, annulment, or abolition."[3] The blood of bulls and goats only **covered** sin. They did not **take it away,** which is why they are only a picture of the better sacrifice that was to come. Old sacrifices freed people from the punishment of sin but not the power of sin. Jesus' sacrifice was different! By His sacrifice, Christ abolished our sin!

> "On the next day John saw Jesus coming toward him and said, 'Look, the Lamb of God who **takes away the sin of the world!**'" (John 1:29)

Stop. Camp right there for a minute and consider that. We sing songs in our churches, raising our hands in praise that we are "covered by the blood," but, in fact, we are more than covered. We say things like, "When God looks at you, He sees you through the lens of Jesus, so He doesn't see your sin." This is also less than what is true. This is the *old* way, covering of our sins, atonement of our sins, and it is less than what we have in Christ. Our sins are not atoned. Our sins have been taken away. We are washed by the blood, fully clean of our sins. When God looks at you, He sees you in fullness, not hiding behind Jesus, but fully united with Christ. All of you and all of Jesus.

Jesus did not get rid of the Law. He didn't destroy it or suddenly change the rules. God always keeps His covenants, and the Law is a covenant. Instead, He completed the Law Covenant on our behalf, making it obsolete, so that we could be free from its regulations, expectations, and limitations and enter into a New Covenant with Him (Hebrews 8). He did this by becoming the

---

[3] James Strong, The New Strong's Exhaustive Concordance of the Bible, Nashville: T. Nelson, 1990, s.v. "*athetésis*"

ultimate, perfect, and willing sacrifice, tearing the veil, and sending God's spirit (His presence) to take up residence in us. He upheld the Law and then took up residence in us so that we have perfection written on our hearts (Hebrews 10:16). It's the blood of Jesus that brings the forgiveness of sins, not our behavior or our confessions. Our forgiveness is defined and sealed by perfect blood, which means we are never anything less than fully forgiven.

> "He has **destroyed what was against us**, a certificate of indebtedness expressed in decrees opposed to us. He has **taken it away** by nailing it to the cross. Disarming the rulers and authorities, he has made a public disgrace of them, triumphing over them by the cross." (Colossians 2:14-15)
>
> "Do not think that I have come to abolish the law or the prophets. **I have not come to abolish these things but to fulfill them.**" (Matthew 5:17)

This atonement sacrifice took place in the Holy of Holies, located inside the temple and entered once a year on the Day of Atonement exclusively by the high priest. This is where the presence of the Lord resided. It was separated from the rest of the temple by a veil that was 4 inches thick, 60 feet high, and 30 feet wide. Inside the Holy of Holies was the Ark of the Covenant, the lid of which was called the Mercy Seat. The Mercy Seat was where the blood of sacrifice was placed on the Day of Atonement by the high priest. God's presence would come and rest on the Mercy Seat as He received the sacrifice offered for the forgiveness of all sins for the nation of Israel. It was considered the holiest of holy places never to be touched by human hands or even looked upon with irreverence.

> **"God publicly displayed him at his death as the mercy seat accessible through faith.** *This was to demonstrate his righteousness, because God in his forbearance had passed over the sins previously committed. This was also to demonstrate his righteousness in the present time, so that he would be just and the justifier of the one who lives"*
> *(Romans 3:25-26)*

Paul writes that God *publicly* displayed Christ as the accessible Mercy Seat. This is a significant and powerful statement that Paul is making. The Mercy Seat was literally the most private and inaccessible place in the temple, kept in complete and total darkness except for on the Day of Atonement. It was off limits, out of reach, and untouchable. The high priest's robes even had bells on them and a rope was tied to his ankle just in case he failed the righteousness test when he approached the Mercy Seat and was struck dead upon entry. The other priests would pull him out by this rope because no one else was allowed to enter the Holy of Holies.

So, you can imagine the audacity of Paul speaking of a public and accessible Mercy Seat! Upon Jesus' death, the veil was torn in two, top to bottom, and the presence of the living God became accessible to all through faith. We can now approach the throne room, not with fear and trepidation as the high priest once did, but with confidence and boldness to receive in fullness all God has to offer!

> *For we do not have a high priest incapable of sympathizing with our weaknesses, but one who has been tempted in every way just as we are, yet*

> *without sin. Therefore, let us **confidently** **approach** the throne of grace to receive mercy and find grace whenever we need help.*
> *(Hebrews 4:15-16)*

What does that mean for us today? It means that we have VIP backstage passes to access God's presence. It means that we get to have something that the ancient Jews never did—the intimate indwelling of Christ's life in us. It means that God is not far away, that He is not some distant entity, but that He is as close as the very breath in our lungs. It means that holiness is no longer hidden in the dark behind closed doors and drawn curtains but now it is a beacon of light constantly beckoning from the human heart that can't help but be seen. Our hearts have become the new Holy of Holies where God's presence lives.

> *"Or do you not know that **your body is the temple of the Holy Spirit who is in you**, whom you have from God, and you are not your own?"*
> *(1 Corinthians 6:19)*

The biggest charge against this gospel of unconditional grace and finished forgiveness is that it's easy on sin or that it overlooks sin. Critics demand we offer a solution to the problem of sin, and I say, we did, it's Jesus. Don't misunderstand me. I'm not saying that sin isn't a problem in our world. I'm not saying that I don't experience struggle. I'm not saying that sin is not damaging or dangerous. I'm saying that sin's wages, its payoff, is death and Christ already died.

Should He be crucified again each time we behave badly? And if Christ already died for that, if He paid that price, settled that debt, why are we so obsessed with the behavior that no longer defines us? Isn't Christ more capable of dealing with sin than I am? Why is it that we want Jesus for our salvation, but we want the moral Law for our sin problem? Have we not read Paul's instruction to the Romans?

> *"Now the **law** came in so that the **transgression may increase**, but where **sin increased, grace multiplied all the more**, so that just as sin reigned in death, so also **grace will reign through righteousness** to eternal life through Jesus Christ our Lord." (Romans 5:20-21)*

Sin seems to be the thing that we talk about most. I mean, just think about it, when was the last time you heard a sermon that didn't talk about some sin or another and how to fix it? How many times do we pray begging God to forgive us of our sins, wondering if He's tired of hearing the same confession over and over again? Our biggest focus in the church is on behavior modification and obedience. We push away and alienate those with "worse sin" than us spouting "love the sinner, hate the sin" as our justification. We talk about it, sing about it, pray about it, preach about it, write about it, and devote our complete focus to it. We let our obsession with it rule and direct our lives either with the purpose of avoiding it or engaging in it. We forget, God doesn't fight dirty.

I write about and teach on the gospel of grace regularly. I repetitively discuss the finished work of Christ, His forgiveness and removal of **all** sins. Countless times I have spoken on the enormity of God's grace that reaches down and grabs us in the midst of our sin and makes us saints (Romans 5:8). Just as many times I have quoted Paul's monologue in Romans 8 that **nothing** can separate us from the love of God in Christ Jesus. Even so, do you know what the most common question people ask me is? The one that I am asked about literally any time I teach about grace? The number one question, the answer that everyone wants to know, is… "What about grace when it comes to _____ sin?"

It absolutely blows my mind at times how people will nod their heads and even let out an excited "amen" at talk of God's great love and favor for us and then with the next breath ask, "But what about when I lie to my boss? But what about when I get angry with my kids? But what about that one guy at church with the porn addiction? But what about *my* past?" Everyone is convinced that their sin is unique, exceptional, and, ultimately, too big for God's grace to overcome. It's incredibly sad really because our obsession with sin keeps our eyes on evil and, in turn, robs us of our focus and freedom to do good. While we're so busy talking about sin, how to manage it, which ones to confess, how to confess them, which ones are unforgivable, and which are acceptable, guess what we're not doing? We're not talking about Jesus.

Jesus, you know, that one guy who is supposedly at the center of our faith. Jesus, the One who took all of our sin upon Himself and carried the weight of it so we wouldn't have to. Jesus, the Deity who put on the fragility of humanity and subjected Himself to the worst pain imaginable for the sole purpose of our redemption. He offers us His divine birthright and, yet, how willing we are to cower at the feet of sin management, our lips wagging in worship of it.

Why is it that we, the church, think our main job is to point out and judge sin? Where did we get that idea anyway? Because last time I checked, that was not our primary charge or our purpose. Last time I checked, it was the job of the Law to measure and reveal sin (Romans 3:20). All over the New Testament we find verses that tell us our job is to encourage one another, to speak in love towards one another, to "edify" (build up) one another. Passage after passage calls us to live in unity because we are all united to Christ through Christ. If you read these verses in context, you will find that, yes, these should result in people leaving their sin, but this is as a *result* of their life in Christ, not a *requirement* of it. Why? Because that's what happens when you have a new heart (Romans 6:17) and live in a community of grace!

The writers of the New Testament call the church to avoid sin, run from sin, and resist sin, not as a way to earn love and closeness with God. Rather, it is because they **have** love and closeness, they are loved perfectly, and that's what perfect love does. If we are teaching one another the truth about who we are in Christ, good behavior will naturally follow from our love for one another.

Jesus demonstrates this to us. In every instance in His time on earth where He says to someone, "Go and sin no more," it is after having shown them great love. See, for an unbeliever, sin is an identity. So, His statement is really a release from bondage not a command of expectation. After encountering Christ, we have freedom! Freedom to do good. Freedom to experience real life. Freedom to have hope in the midst of despair.

---

> *"And having been **freed from sin**, you became enslaved to righteousness. For just as you once*

> *presented your members as slaves to impurity and lawlessness leading to more lawlessness, so now* **present your members as slaves to righteousness** *leading to sanctification. For when you were slaves of sin, you were free with regard to righteousness." (Romans 6:18-20)*

Many could misunderstand me and think that I am saying we should ignore sin. This misunderstanding comes from a limited view of what grace really is. As we discussed in the first chapter, most view grace as being solely about forgiveness, Jesus' blood that covers our failures. And grace most certainly is *big* forgiveness. Complete forgiveness is an extravagant and exciting part of grace, but grace is so much more than that. God is much bigger than our expectations or deserving efforts. He doesn't just stop at forgiveness. He also offers us new life, and this life is the very life of Christ in us. We get a completely new identity that is interwoven in Christ's identity and with it comes new desires and motivations.

Paul tells the young pastor, Titus, that **grace** is what trains us in godliness (Titus 2:11-12). The reason that the message of grace is so radical is that it teaches us to live out of Christ in us, not to just go out and participate in sin recklessly. In other words, I now have new passions and desires that come from the perfect Spirit of Christ pumping in my veins. What could sin possibly give to me that would offer any lasting satisfaction?

> *"So* **what benefit did you then reap from those things that you are now ashamed of***? For the end of those things is death. But now, freed from*

> *sin and enslaved to God,* **you have your benefit leading to sanctification, and the end is eternal life.** *For the payoff of sin is death, but the gift of God is eternal life in Christ Jesus our Lord."*
> *(Romans 6:21-23)*

---

My desperate prayer for the church is that it finds freedom from a sin-focused life. May it come to realize and believe that even the darkest and dirtiest of sins has already been judged, punished, and paid for by Christ. And may this belief be the foundation for lives overwhelmed by God's scandalous grace.

## An Opposing Doctrine: Forgiveness Through Continued Confession

Unfortunately, the idea of finished forgiveness is not the only boxer in the ring. In the opposite corner, stands the church's reigning champion, continued confession. This doctrine takes many forms and goes by many names. The most subtle and simple of which is the idea that when you sin, you need to pray and ask God to forgive you every time.

Most people cite 1 John 1:9 as their proof text for this continued confession doctrine. **"But if we confess our sins, he is faithful and righteous forgiving us our sins and cleansing us from all unrighteousness."** I am going to cover this specific passage in greater detail later in the book but let me give you a little summarized spoiler. This passage is not a passage written to Christians as instruction on the daily asking for and receiving of forgiveness for every new sin. This passage, in context, is written to *unbelievers*. It is addressed to those who are actively denying sin, calling God a liar, and are *different* from those who have accepted the cleansing of Jesus' blood. This is an evangelistic instructional passage on how to *become* a Christian, not instructions for those of us who already are.

Now, hold on just a minute before you go running to get the tar and feathers. I am *not* saying that sin doesn't necessitate forgiveness. It does, and Jesus did it. I am *not* saying that sin isn't deadly and dangerous. It is, and it killed Him. I am *not* saying we shouldn't turn away from sin. We should, and He empowers us to.

What *am* I saying?

I am saying what Paul said. We mindlessly quote the verse like a lyric to our favorite song and in the same way pay no attention to the words we say, marketing belief systems opposed to it.

> "**For the wages of sin is death**, but the gift of God
> is eternal life in Christ Jesus our Lord."
> *(Romans 6:23 NIV)*
>
> "For the **payoff of sin is death**, but the gift of God
> is eternal life in Christ Jesus our Lord."
> *(Romans 6:23 NET)*

The cost of sin is death. The cost of sin is not distance from God. The cost of sin is not "broken fellowship." The cost of sin is not God being sad. The cost of sin is **death**. Therefore, the payment for sin is not confession. The payment for sin is not promised commitment to doing better.  The payment for sin is not pleading for mercy over and over.  The payment for sin is not a pledge of better behavior.  The payment for sin is not asking for forgiveness.

Imagine you make your weekly grocery run to Walmart.  You load up your cart with all your food for the week, necessities for life, and favorite snacks.  Full cart in tow, you make your way up to the checkout line.  The cashier rings up all your items and says, "Your total is $113.73."  Now imagine you pull out your wallet, and, thumbing through your billfold, you pull out two bright yellow pieces of paper inked with the symbol 100.  Monopoly money you grabbed on your way out the door.  Cheerfully you hand it to the cashier, "Here you go.  You can keep the change!"  How far do you think you'd get out of the parking lot with your groceries before red and blue flashing lights appear in your rearview?

Of course, this is ludicrous.  You can't pay for groceries with Monopoly money because, unfortunately, that's not an accepted currency anywhere in the world except for your living room.  You cannot pay for your sins with your words, works, or want-to's.  Covenant currency is blood.  All other payment methods are declined.

> "Indeed according to the law almost everything was purified with blood, and **without the shedding of blood there is no forgiveness.**"
> *(Hebrews 9:22)*

Forgiveness isn't free because it doesn't cost anything—it's free because someone already paid for it.  It was purchased with the priceless and innocent blood of Jesus who was guilty of nothing but loving us. Let us become more aware of that scandalous truth, that the most expensive gift has been freely given to us. It was bought at a high price, the blood of One who loved us more than we can ever imagine when we least deserved it. This price has been paid in full so that we might enjoy it free of charge! Forgiveness cannot be put on layaway, making a payment every paycheck with each confession, hoping one day we get to enjoy what we worked so hard for. It is ours, in fullness, right now.

---

*"You know that from your empty way of life inherited from your ancestors you were ransomed—**not by perishable things like silver or gold, but by precious blood** like that of an unblemished and spotless lamb, namely Christ."*
*(1 Peter 1:18-19)*

---

*Sure, sure, sure, but what about repentance? The Bible <u>clearly</u> says we need to repent!*

The Greek word for repentance is **metánoia** which literally means, "a change of mind."[4] To repent is simply to change your mind. Sure, believers can and should repent from sin, meaning, they should change their mind about sin. In other words, renew your mind to believe the truth. Change your mind and believe that sin is of no benefit to you. Change your mind and believe that you're not a slave to sin. Change your mind and believe that goodness is at the core of who you are, and you don't actually want to sin.

---

[4] James Strong, The New Strong's Exhaustive Concordance of the Bible, Nashville: T. Nelson, 1990, s.v. " metánoia"

Change your mind from old ways of thinking that don't align with truth.

Repentance for the believer is simply about adjusting your belief system, not about begging for forgiveness. In scripture, when this word is used in reference to *forgiveness*, this is always used to describe conversion, turning towards Christ for salvation, the forgiveness of sins. Repentance for forgiveness, yeah, do that. Please do that. And if you're reading this now as a believer, guess what? You did! No matter which way you look at it, the fact of the matter is when it comes to the forgiveness of your sins, in the words of Jesus, it's finished.

> *"Therefore repent and return, **so that your sins may be wiped away**, in order that times of refreshing may come from the presence of the Lord." (Acts 3:19)*
>
> *"Peter said to them, 'Repent, and each of you be baptized in the name of Jesus Christ **for the forgiveness of your sins**; and you will receive the gift of the Holy Spirit.'" (Acts 2:38)*

Why does this distinction matter? If we believe that God's action is dependent on our contrition or confession, then we are disregarding the cross. We are saying that Jesus wasn't enough and that God needs more in order to be satisfied. And if Jesus wasn't enough for God, how could we ever believe that God has anything good for us? If Jesus wasn't enough, then God breaks His promises. If our forgiveness isn't finished and final, then we might as well just close the curtain on this whole Christianity thing.

If we adjust our thinking to align with the truth that we are fully forgiven, then we are free to approach our relationship with Him with gratitude instead of fear. When we fall short in our behavior, as we inevitably will, instead of anxiously begging Him to forgive us, we can joyfully thank Him that He already has. This empowers us to confidently approach Him when we need help, knowing that we will only ever find mercy and grace in His presence. What if, instead of begging God for forgiveness next time you sin, you thanked Him for what He already provided instead? Maybe then your relationship with Him would be rooted in gratitude and not anxiety. Maybe then you would find yourself depending on His power to save you rather than your efforts to be saved.

Divine forgiveness is bigger and better than we ever imagined, but it is still only half of the salvation story. Because God is excessive and extreme with His love for us, salvation contains both forgiveness of our sins and a new life empowered by His Spirit.

# New Life

RUINING THE RELIGION OF KILLING YOURSELF

The symbol of the cross is the most recognized image in Christian iconography and has become the most used identifier for Christians across the globe.  You find it on t-shirts, signs, buildings, and plastered across Christian merchandise.  Those wanting to clearly identify themselves as Christians wear it around their necks, stick it on their cars, and maybe even tattoo it across their backs.  In many ways, the cross has become the logo of Christian branding.

I did an experiment once and asked over 100 Christians from a variety of denominations, "What does the cross represent to you personally?"  The answer in the overwhelming majority was some version of "Jesus forgave me" or "Jesus died for my sins."  While I don't believe that this answer is a bad answer or a wrong answer, it is an incomplete answer.  To explain what I mean, let's take a look at a passage from the book of Romans.

> *"So then, just as sin entered the world through one man and **death through sin**, and so **death spread to all people** because all sinned— for before the law was given, sin was in the world, but there is no accounting for sin when there is no law. **Yet death reigned from Adam until Moses** even over those who did not sin in the same way that Adam (who is a type of the coming one) transgressed. But the gracious gift is not like the transgression. For if the many died through the transgression of the one man, how much more did the grace of God and the gift by the grace of the one man Jesus Christ multiply to the many! And the gift is not like the one who sinned. For judgment, resulting from the one transgression, led to condemnation, but the gracious gift from the many failures led to justification. **For if, by the transgression of the one man, death reigned through the one, how much more will those who receive the abundance of grace and of the gift of righteousness reign in life through the one, Jesus Christ!** Consequently, just as condemnation for all people came through one transgression, so too through the one righteous act came **righteousness leading to life for all people**."*
> *(Romans 5:12-18)*

There is a glaring truth found in this passage that, as evidenced by my survey, goes largely unnoticed by the modern church today. When Adam partook in the fruit of tree, it was not only sin that entered his heart but also death. Now, I'm not talking about physical death here necessarily, but rather spiritual death.

Adam took in the knowledge of good and evil and it literally murdered him from the inside out. God warned Adam that this would happen back in chapter 2 of Genesis. ***"But you must not eat from the tree of the knowledge of good and evil, for when you eat from it <u>you will surely die</u>." (Genesis 2:17)*** Adam did, in fact, die, and that death was a spiritual death. So, we can see that there is a dual nature to the fall of man: sin and death.

I love a good sci-fi, monster, or dystopian horror film. This is especially true if the movie has anything to do with cryptids or zombies. We've come a long way from *Night of the Living Dead* and now have hundreds of different iterations of zombies. We have crazy end-of-the-world virus zombies, spores that take over your brain zombies, voodoo zombies, and we even have zombies who fall in love (don't get me started on that one). While there are plenty of different zombie versions, one thing they all agree on, and what zombies are most known for, is their unquenchable appetite. All they ever do is try to consume the living, and they won't stop until they do. They will eat and eat and eat and never be satisfied because they are zombies and that's what zombies do.

Before Christ, we are essentially spiritual zombies. We look like we're alive. We move from place to place. We interact with the world. Yet, we are dead inside, driven only by the satisfaction of our appetites. We try desperately to consume things that look like life if only to quiet our hunger pangs for another hour or so. We can see nothing and no one outside of ourselves. We sin against ourselves and each other and God because we're zombies and that's what zombies do.

Forgiveness alone doesn't do much to heal our spiritual deadness. So, we can see, because there is a duality of nature in the fall, there must be a duality of nature in salvation in order for redemption to take place: forgiveness and life.

You know the problem with the Church today? We only preach half of the gospel. We want to talk about forgiveness and the cross all day long, which is great. Don't get me wrong, we'd be hopeless beings were it not for the mercy of forgiveness, but that's only half of the story. See, because not only was our sin defeated with Christ's last breath on that cross, but *His* spiritual life was provided to us as He kicked down death's door and busted out of the tomb. The gospel is incomplete without the glorious grace of Christ's life *in* us. The resurrection proves that Christ defeated sin and death.

> *"And although **you were dead in your offenses** and sins, in which you formerly lived according to this world's present path, according to the ruler of the domain of the air, the ruler of the spirit that is now energizing the sons of disobedience, among whom all of us also formerly lived out our lives in the cravings of our flesh, indulging the desires of the flesh and the mind, and were by nature children of wrath even as the rest...*
>
> *But God, being rich in mercy, because of his great love with which he loved us, **even though we were dead in offenses, made us alive together with Christ**—by grace you are saved— and he raised us up together with him and seated us together with him in the heavenly realms in Christ Jesus, to*

> *demonstrate in the coming ages the surpassing*
> *wealth of his grace in kindness toward us in Christ*
> *Jesus. (Ephesians 1:1-7)*

---

In the midst of the decay, the grunge, grime, and rank odor of your decomposing spirit, you were overwhelmed and overtaken by the glory and grace of life so that though you were once a zombie seeking only the next piece of flesh that would satisfy your unquenchable appetite, you have now been made alive and vibrant in Christ. You are free to no longer live solely for your next meal but to feast and be filled with all that you could ever wish for or need.

It's interesting to me that within Christianity we readily accept that through one man (Adam) sin distributed to all of humanity, but some doubt that through one God (Christ) salvation was made accessible to all. I mean, could we really call God just if by one man's choice all were condemned but by One's sacrifice only the chosen or "elected" are offered salvation? No. We are *all* presented with the same choice as Adam.

Just as Adam had to take in the fruit of the tree for sin and death to inhabit him, so also must we take in the fruit of salvation (that is Christ) to be inhabited by forgiveness and life. Will we choose to grasp at independence under the guise of god-likeness or will we rest in dependence on the heart of God-life in us?

If you have chosen the latter, then you have made the better choice! You were once a zombie in Adam, and now you are alive in Christ. This is a beautiful picture of God's heart for redemption and the gift of the empty tomb! Let's just look at some different things that happened with Adam's sin and Jesus's death and see how different they are.

- Lamb killed to make Adam's clothes- **Death** (Genesis 3:21)
- Bodies rose up out of their graves at Jesus death- **Life** (Matthew 27:52)
- Adam kicked out of the garden- **Separation** from God's presence (Genesis 3:24)
- Jesus tore the veil- **Access** to God's presence (Mark 15:38)

Our resurrection in Christ also comes with better benefits.

- In Adam, we have **shame**. In Christ, we have **honor**. (Genesis 3:7; 1 Peter 2:9)
- In Adam, we have **distance**. In Christ, we have **unity**. (Genesis 3:23; 1 Corinthians 6:17)
- In Adam, we have **struggle through effort**. In Christ, we have **all that we need for life and godliness.** (Genesis 3:19; 2 Peter 1:3)

I'm certain that Paul continually contrasts Adam and Jesus throughout his writing to show us all the differences between what man's efforts earn us and what God's action freely gives us. Is not Christ far superior? With His death, He bought life, while we, with our lives, earned death. And so, He pays our debt before we can even finish creating it.

Christ came not only to forgive us but also to raise us from the dead. It comes down to this, we need life. Without it we have no choice but to do dead things because that's what dead people do.

Sin is a dead thing. That means it has no claim to rule over those of us who have life. By imparting His life to us, Christ enables us to walk in victory, living full, free, and no longer under the power of sin.

> *"For the love of Christ controls us, having concluded this, that one died for all, therefore all died; and He died for all, so that those who live would no longer live for themselves, but for Him who died and rose on their behalf."*
> *(2 Corinthians 5:14-15 NASB)*

He was killed on a hill called "Golgotha." It means, "Place of the Skull," truly an image of death. The Place of the Skull, where death ruled, where terror reigned as Roman soldiers hoisted broken bodies of the burglars and the battle scarred. The Place of the Skull where the stench of stagnant blood stung nostrils and the shrill of bereavement's cry deafened ears. THIS is where Jesus chose to stretch wide his arms and take on the world's sin and death, our sin and death.

There, at the Place of the Skull, when all who watched believed that death had won; glorious, unquenchable, relentless love gave birth to life. And not just any life, not this fleeting vapor in the wind thing that we call life, but a beautiful eternal life for all who would choose to breathe it in.

That's what I love about God, where others expect death, He births life. When others see dirt, He breathes life. When others see a barren womb, He creates life. When others expect famine, He creates life because He is God and that's what God does.

So, there at that place, the Place of the Skull, where death had reigned for so long, He defeated it for the rest of eternity. In that moment, He not only vanquished death but caressed our spirits and brought them to life.

So now we live, as spirits overwhelmed with life, desperately trying not to burst the seams of this shell we wear, this skin that confines us, this skull that makes us think we are fragile. It would do us well to remember that we are spirits occupying a body and not the other way around. Let us remember that, and that we have power, power beyond what we can even begin to comprehend fueled by a spirit infused with the very resurrection life of Christ.

This is the fullness of the complete gospel. The cross killed our sinful self, and the resurrection brought us a new life.

> "For God achieved what the law could not do because it was weakened through the flesh. By sending his own Son in the likeness of sinful flesh **and concerning sin, he condemned sin in the flesh, so that the righteous requirement of the law may be fulfilled in us**, who do not walk according to the flesh but according to the Spirit."
> (Romans 8:3-4)

## An Opposing Doctrine: Die to Self

Living in the heart of the Bible belt means that I am surrounded on every corner by churches. In the small Texas town where I live, we have more churches per capita than Whataburgers, which honestly is impressive. As is the modern American way, these churches are very invested in advertising their services in various forms, including flyers distributed to all the addresses in the area.

One early morning as I flipped though the various junk mail stuffed into my mailbox, one church's flyer grabbed my attention. On it was this verse, **"Then he said to them all, 'If anyone wants to become my follower, he must deny himself, take up his cross daily, and follow me.'"** That is Luke 9:23, a verse I have heard probably 50 to 100 times in my life and, at one time, believed it to mean exactly what the flyer said it meant. **"Jesus makes it very clear that unless you are willing to deny yourself and take up your cross daily, you cannot be His disciple."** It went on to talk about the cross as an instrument of death and our responsibility to sacrifice daily and die to ourselves daily as our way of seeking to please God.

This is not a new or groundbreaking interpretation of this scripture, and it is one I have spent a lifetime hearing. In fact, there was a time that I used to believe similarly. There was a time when I would have even passionately defended that mindset, although all I found in it was emptiness. If your goal is to please God by sacrificing yourself, I have news for you... you will fail every single time. The point of the cross was for Christ's sacrifice to make us right, to set us free, and to bring us life. The point of Him taking on the cross was so that we don't have to.

Religious teaching has taken verses like this one in Luke (or its buddies in Mark and Matthew) and built an entirely false, but common, doctrine on it called "dying to self." Did you know that exact phrase is not found anywhere in the Bible? That's right. In all 66 books of the Old and New Testament, it's nowhere to be found.  In Romans 6, Paul tells us to consider ourselves dead to **sin**.  Later in Romans and again in Galatians, he reminds us we are dead to the **Law**, but you will not find the phrase "die to self" anywhere in scripture.

I'd like to give those who cling to this perspective the benefit of the doubt and assume that their intention is to try to convey a call to Christians to set aside behaviors of selfishness, self-focus, and self-righteousness.  Honestly, even if that is their intention, that phrase doesn't actually communicate what they intend.  What most people really hear when they hear that phrase is not "give up selfishness."  What they hear when they hear that phrase is, "Your self is bad.  You are gross and icky and can't be trusted no matter what."

For the religious, this leads to more effort, more striving, more sacrifice, and more measuring.  It makes them committed to identifying, measuring, and comparing their sin to those around them, resulting in a soul fixated on judgment and, for the honest ones, ends in burnout and exhaustion.  For the rebels, this leads to giving up on goodness and,  instead, chasing what they think is freedom down rabbit trails littered with fake gratification.  This results in a soul fixated on temporary highs, unsatisfying pleasures, shameful regrets, and, for the honest ones, feelings of misery.  This doctrine of "die to self" feeds a mindset that is either self-righteous or self-loathing, thus creating the very thing it attempts to prevent.

For me personally, this message of spiritual suicide has been a deadly doctrine.  Though I have walked down both paths in my time on this planet, I've spent a lot more time in my life being self-loathing than self-righteous. I have to be incredibly intentional about viewing myself through the truth of God's eyes and not my own shame. My mind has to be continually renewed into believing that who I am in Christ is enough. And so, when I read verses like 1 Corinthians 5:17, which says, **"So then, if anyone is in Christ, he is a new creation; what is old has passed away—look, what is new has come,"** I am filled with relief and hope in the truth that I'm something new now! I don't have to hate myself because I am a sparkling, new, beautiful creation in Christ.

So, when religion comes to us with that phrase, "die to self," we have to stop and say, but wait a second. I thought Paul just said I was a new creation. Why do I need to die again? Didn't Christ do that already?

Let's take another look at our Luke passage, but now with verse 24 added in for more context. **"Then he said to them all, 'If anyone wants to <u>become my follower</u>, he must deny himself, take up his cross daily, and follow me. For whoever wants to save his life will lose it, but whoever loses his life for my sake will save it.'"** What if Jesus' point was not for us to be crucified daily, do enough daily, or nail ourselves with guilt when we fail? Jesus' statement here is made to His disciples, immediately after they have identified Him as the Messiah. With this statement, He is giving them instructions on how to become a follower of Christ. Jesus is foreshadowing what is coming. Remember, they don't yet know how this story ends. It is still being written for them. They don't know that crucifixion is coming.

The call into following Christ is to deny our pre-saved selves (our efforts, our sacrifices, our expectations, and our duties) opting instead for His sacrifice, the ultimate sacrifice, that was enough. Maybe that's why He goes on to say that if we try to save our life ourselves, we will lose it. We must be crucified with Christ in order to have a new, eternal life. And we already were! (Galatians 2:20)

This is really an evangelistic passage and Jesus' call to His disciples to trust in Him for salvation. Unlike those disciples, we have the incredible gift and privilege to live on the "it is finished" side of the cross. We have become more than just "followers" of Christ. We are one with Him and are therefore God's kids . We have a new self that is full of righteousness and holiness (Ephesians 4:22-24). When we let go and accept His life in us as the only way to please God, we enter into the only true discipleship—life in Christ.

There is so much peace out there for you if you just stop trying to gain something that you already have. There is rest from the weariness of sacrifice. There is hope from the brokenness of self-effort and failure. There is freedom from the reality of unmet expectations. You are incredibly, unconditionally, and incomparably loved by God. You can stop trying to murder what God resurrected.

# Complete Closeness

RUINING THE RELIGION OF DAMAGED CONNECTION

The very first lie that Satan ever told us was that God is withholding and distant. It's clever, really, because it taps into something we instinctively know to be true, which is that God is different than us. Not only do we know He's different, but, of course, we also know He is bigger and better than us. Adam and Eve probably knew this intimately as people who walked with God and learned His character. Thus, Satan's ingenious deception for mankind was not for us to move towards evil, but rather to grip God's goodness for ourselves. The temptation was for independent god-likeness made more enticing by a promise that we could be closer to Him if we had it.

Satan has not learned any new tricks in the last half-dozen millennia. The same lie weaves its way into our minds, validated by a religion that talks far more about God's power and holiness than about His love. We still know, instinctively, that God is far bigger, holier, and more powerful than us. We boast of His sovereignty, throwing the term around casually in our church circles.

When the word "sovereign" is used in the church, it is most often used as a term to describe the bigness and power of God. It's this idea that God is in control of every miniscule aspect of life as we know it—that He knows all things and oversees all things. For me, use of the word "sovereign" always had this air of coldness about it. You know what I mean? Like discussion of "God's sovereignty" always lacked intimacy or connection and mostly made God seem to me like an overseer or distant watcher rather than a personal God.

Coupled with that was lots of talk about God's will. Find God's will, stay in God's will, pray for God's will, watch out or you'll be out of God's will. Make sure you marry the right person, take the right job, buy the right house, and move to the right city. In summary, God's big and in charge and if you don't figure out His secret plan and stay in it, then, sure, you might have an okay life, but you'll certainly never have a *great* life. This makes God out to be some distant, boxed-in, linear thinker and, frankly, pretty small, if you ask me. When it comes to God, that's not at all what sovereignty looks like. A truly sovereign God is both transcendent and intimate.

By "transcendent," I mean that He exists above, outside of, and apart from our limitations or the limitations of our universe. By "intimate," I mean that He is tangled up and a part of the smallest parts of our lives. He is infinitely big and infinitely small.

There is this weird paradox where God is outside of and also in the middle of all things. We see this about God as far back as the creation story. He speaks all creation into existence with a distant word and then, when He gets to man, He puts His hands in the dirt and intimately breathes life into us. He is intangible and yet He touches our softest parts.

> *"He is the image of the invisible God, the firstborn over all creation, for all things in heaven and on earth were created in him—all things, whether visible or invisible, whether thrones or dominions, whether principalities or powers—all things were created through him (intimate) and for him (transcendent). He himself is before all things (transcendent) and all things are held together in him (intimate). He is the head of the body, the church, as well as the beginning, the firstborn from the dead, so that he himself may become first in all things. (transcendent). For God was pleased to have all his fullness dwell in the Son and through him to reconcile all things to himself by making peace through the blood of his cross—through him, whether things on earth or things in heaven. (intimate)"*
> *(Colossians 1:15-20, parentheses added)*

It seems that God is in no *need* of relationship with us, yet, He still seeks to initiate one with us. God knew how hard it would be for us to relate to Him, to know Him and His heart for us, because He does far transcend our understanding. He also witnessed us constantly struggling to allow Him to come close despite His persistent attempts at drawing near to us. And so, in that knowledge, God, initiating intimacy, entered our world and became relatable.

> *"In the beginning was the Word, and the Word was with God, and the Word was fully God. The Word was with God in the beginning. All things were created by him, and apart from him not one thing was created that has been created (transcendent). In him was life (intimate), and the life was the light of mankind. And the light shines on in the darkness, but the darkness has not mastered it."*
> (John 1:1-5, parentheses added)

How can we know an intangible God that far transcends our reality if not for His intimate invasion into our space? Not only did He do this in the physical person of Jesus, but also, we find that He has twisted Himself up in us and actively seeks to speak directly to our hearts in the language that we best understand. I believe that if we allow ourselves to live in awareness of this, we might just fall even more deeply in love with God and discover the amazing true reality of an intimate life with Him.

I learned in Sunday school as far back as I can remember that when I accepted Christ as my Savior, He came to live in my heart, which is absolutely true. Galatians teaches us that part of being God's child means having the Spirit of His Son in our hearts (Galatians 4:6). This idea of Jesus coming to live in our hearts makes for a great, simplistic way to teach children about salvation, but as we mature in our understanding, there is more for us to know about the depth of what that salvation life really looks like.

> *"For if we have become **united with him** in the likeness of his death, we will certainly also be **united** in the likeness of his resurrection. We know that our old man was crucified with him so that the body of sin would no longer dominate us, so that we would no longer be enslaved to sin. For someone who has died has been freed from sin."*
> *(Romans 6:5-7)*
>
> *"For the one **united** with the Lord is **one** spirit with Him."* *(1 Corinthians 6:17)*

For a very long time, I missed the depth of what Paul is saying here about being united with Christ. In a very small way, because of my childhood Christ occupancy lessons, I understood the idea of Christ being in *me*, but for most of my life, my understanding stopped there and I never was able to wrap my mind around the idea of *me* being in *Christ*. Paul says here that we are *united* with Christ.

Think about it like this: Imagine a pitcher of water. It's perfectly clear, fresh and clean. Now imagine that someone was to add blue food coloring to the water and mix it up. The water now becomes a deep blue. Can you distinguish between what is water and what is blue food coloring? Can you separate the two? Well, no, of course not. Now it's just blue water because the food coloring and water have united as one. This is how it is with us and Christ. He doesn't just come into our hearts and we remain separate entities, but rather, He injects Himself into our fundamental being, at the deepest level of our identity, and we become something different, united as one, inseparable, and a new thing altogether.

The Greek word used here for "united" is the word **sumphutos,** which is an adjective meaning "congenital, innate, implanted by birth or nature, born together with."[5] Do you see what I am getting at here? When we are united with Christ, our innate, from-birth nature is changed. In fact, it's not just changed, but it's made one with the birth nature of Christ! I don't know about you, but I find that to be a big reality to wrap my mind around.

And this reality takes us a step further because, think about this, if I were to take our pitcher of blue water and pour it down the sink, what would happen to the blue food coloring? What about the water? They would both go down the sink. Why? Because they are one entity. Now, what if I were to take that pitcher and put it in the fridge? Would both the blue food coloring and the water get cold? Yes, of course, because they are one! So, if this represents us and Christ and we are in Christ and Christ is in us and we are one, then what happens when Christ dies to sin? Don't we also die to sin? And if He is raised to new life that is teeming with righteousness and holiness, aren't we also raised to that life? And if He is seated in heavenly places, aren't we?

> *"But God, being rich in mercy, because of his great love with which he loved us, even though we were dead in offenses, made us alive together with Christ—by grace you are saved!* ***and he raised us up together with him and seated us together with him in the heavenly realms in Christ Jesus.****" (Ephesians 2:1-6)*

---

[5] James Strong, The New Strong's Exhaustive Concordance of the Bible, Nashville: T. Nelson, 1990, s.v. "*sumphutos* "

Jesus prayed for this oneness to happen to all that believe in Him. He prayed not only for us to be united but that our unity would be the same level of unity that He and the Father share with one another. Now, just stop for a moment and consider that. You are as united to Christ as Jesus is to God the Father, the same level of unity. An equal measure of closeness as Jesus and God have with each other. In essence, you have been inserted into divine community. You can't get any closer than that!

---

> *"I am not praying only on their behalf, but also on behalf of those who believe in me through their testimony, that they **will all be one, just as you, Father, are in me and I am in you**. I pray **that they will be in us**, so that the world will believe that you sent me. The glory you gave to me I have given to them, that **they may be one just as we are one**— I in them and you in me—that they may be completely one, so that the world will know that you sent me, and you have loved them just as you have loved me." (John 17:20-23)*

> *"For in him all the fullness of deity lives in bodily form, and **you have been filled in him,** who is the head over every ruler and authority" (Colossians 2:9-10)*

---

What if the reality is that we are constantly drenched in the presence of God? What if we are dripping wet in His glory and we are too busy looking for a way to get closer to be in awe of it. May it never be that we miss the reality of His ever-presentness while we are distracted by our own limitations. May it never be that we become too preoccupied with cleaning up our corner of the world that we miss God right there in our everyday precious things.

I guess the point I'm trying to make is that God is right now, in this moment and all the ones that follow, eagerly initiating intimacy with you. He is speaking your language, whatever it sounds like, whether it's grandeur or simplicity. God is right now wrapped up in you. Right now.  Only a sovereign God can do that. That's what sovereignty really means.

I wasted a lot of time believing that God was cold and distant and angry. Even if He wasn't angry, He surely wasn't concerned with the language of my heart or my expression.  I have often believed He behaves as humans would, but this belief just doesn't line up with the God of the Bible who we find over and over again initiating intimacy with us exactly where we are.

> *"By this the love of God was revealed in us, that God has sent His only Son into the world so that we may live through Him.* **In this is love, not that we loved God, but that He loved us** *and sent His Son to be the propitiation for our sins."*
> *(1 John 4:9-10 NASB)*

I encourage you to allow yourself to experience a God who speaks your language, who is willing to get all up in your personal space. Know that God is intimately intertwined in your every day, in the very breath you take without realizing it, and that there is nothing you can do to make yourself any less worth the intimacy to Him. There's also nothing you can do to make yourself *more* worth it. You are as close as you ever will be to Him, fully united.

> *"For you have died and your life is hidden **with Christ in God**. When Christ (who is your life) appears, then you too will be revealed **in glory with him**. (Colossians 3:3-4)*

This is the good news gospel of God for the believer: He is for us. He is bigger than us and, yet, He takes up residence in the smallest parts of our hearts. He speaks words of affection into our softest, most vulnerable places.

In that Romans 6 passage we looked at earlier, Paul reveals the results of this closeness. Just as the death which reigns supreme in this world has no right to boss Christ around, neither does it have that right with us. Because this is true about us, we should no longer live our lives participating in dead things and being bullied by sin. This no longer lines up with our new birth nature. It's uncomfortable. It's fleeting and unsatisfying. It's not who we are anymore! We have died to sin with Christ and have a new self, a new heart, a new identity that is enveloped in the very nature of Jesus!

Without the righteousness of Christ in us, working for us; without the intimate and personal person of God entering our broken spaces; without the stubborn grace of God seeking us out and sabotaging the wickedness of the human heart; without these things, we are utterly hopeless in fighting our sin. Without God, we live in bondage to the very acts that make us cringe while reading them. The good news is, we not only never again have to worry about being without Him, but also, that we are so close to Him that we are one. May we live in constant awareness both of our desperate need for His presence and the new reality that we are always in it.

## An Opposing Doctrine: Damaged Fellowship

The idea that the God of the universe is united in oneness with us fragile humans is a complex concept for us to wrap our minds around. I would venture to say that it is as big and difficult to fully understand as the concept of the Trinity, which has been argued about and wrestled with by well-educated Christians for centuries. It's a heaven concept, not of this world, alien in a way, and so we humans have a hard time taking it in. Add to that the reality that we often *feel* distant from God, especially when we make mistakes, and we end up with a religion manufactured doctrine of damaged fellowship.

Have you noticed how infatuated we Christians are with chopping up the gospel? It's true! We start splitting things up and putting them in Christianese packaging in an attempt to reconcile what we *feel* with what God says is true about us. Don't believe me? Here are some examples.

- You've accepted Christ as your **Savior**, but have you made Him **Lord**?
- We have **positional** righteousness but not **practical** righteousness.
- God sees you as **holy**, but also you are being **progressively made more holy** here on earth.
- You're **saved**, but have you entered His **rest**?
- Our **relationship** with God is never broken because He loves us unconditionally, but our **fellowship** with Him is damaged when we sin.

I want to focus in on the last one in that list as it relates to our oneness with God. It is the most frustrating one to me because, quite honestly, it's just stupid. The word "fellowship" and the word "relationship" are literally synonyms. Okay. Sure, you could argue that fellowship is the action or living out of relationship, but even so, they are connected to each other. Listen, I'm no linguist, but I can at least use my common sense about the English language to see that this is an illogical split of terms.

Let's set aside for a minute my hang-up with the language piece of this and pretend that relationship and fellowship are different things. In the New Testament, depending on what version of the Bible you are using, the word "fellowship" appears around 20 times in reference to Christians. Of those, most are in reference to believers' fellowship with one another, calling us to be connected and enjoy relationship with each other in the body of Christ. However, there are a few that reference our fellowship with Christ or with the Spirit, typically as part of a blessing or prayer given by the author to those reading the letter. Here's my personal favorite:

> *"For you were **made rich in every way in him**, in all your speech and in every kind of knowledge, just as the testimony about Christ has been confirmed among you, so that **you do not lack any spiritual gift** as you wait for the revelation of our Lord Jesus Christ. He will also strengthen you to the end, so that you will be blameless on the day of our Lord Jesus Christ. **God is faithful, by whom you were called into fellowship with his Son**, Jesus Christ our Lord." (1 Corinthians 1:5-9)*

That verse certainly doesn't seem to indicate that our fellowship with Christ is in danger of being broken. In fact, it communicates that our fellowship with Christ is without lack and dependent on God's faithfulness, not our behavior.

The most common verse that is used to imply that *Christians* who are one with Christ could be out of fellowship with Him is found in 1 John 1:6. **"If we say we have fellowship with him and yet keep on walking in the darkness, we are lying and not practicing the truth."** At face value, taking the verse completely on its own, I can see why some would interpret this to mean that we can fall in and out of fellowship with God based on if we are walking in light or darkness. However, if what we have learned is true, and is evidenced repeatedly across the whole of scripture, about God being united in fullness with us, then that interpretation of this one scripture cannot be correct. If our interpretation of a verse contradicts multiple other verses across scripture, then we should reconsider our understanding of the passage. This is a great example of why reading scripture in context matters.

We established earlier that I was a fiery kid, a handful to say the least. As a child, I was a loud, curious, fireball of passion, who made a ruckus and climbed trees onto the church roof and corrected her Sunday School teachers. I was pretty sure I knew everything and that all adults were pretty dumb and should just listen to me and my obvious wisdom. My dad used to say I was "full of dangerous wonder." My mom would have said I was full of… other things. As you can imagine, this made raising me… well… less than boring.

One day my mom and I got into an argument about something small, I'm sure (it didn't take much back then), resulting in me exploding in anger and Mom sending me to my room to "think about my choices." I was about 11 years old at the time and, again, certain I knew everything. I got the bright idea that I was going to get Mom back and make her feel bad about the clear injustice she was bestowing upon me. Being the good baby legalist that I was, I grabbed my Bible in search of a verse with which to shame her. At last, I found it and plastered a smug smirk on my face as I marched back into the kitchen to read Mom her rights. "Mom," I accused angrily, "you are not being a good Christian parent right now. It says so right here in the Bible!" I then proceeded to proudly and dramatically read off my scripture. Ephesians 6:4, **"Do not provoke your children to anger, but raise them up in the discipline and instruction of the Lord."** Then, I looked up at her victoriously. What could she possibly say to that, after all? She turned to me, lowered her voice calmly, and answered, "What does the verse above it say?"

*The verse above it? Uh... I... wait a second.*

Suddenly deflated, I looked down at the Bible in my hands and began to read, **"Children, obey your parents in the Lord, for this is right. Honor your father and mother—this is the first commandment with a promise: So that it may go well with you and that you may live a long life on the earth."**

At only 11 years old, I already found myself falling for the oldest religious trap: weaponizing a verse taken out of context. Thankfully, I learned my lesson from that little escapade, and though I got many more things wrong in years to come, weaponizing a verse out of context typically wasn't one of them. Unfortunately, it seems that some of us have not quite learned that lesson yet. Let's not be like 11-year-old Jess and instead look at our 1 John verse in full context

> "Now this is the gospel message we have heard from him and announce to you: God is light, and in him there is no darkness at all. If we say we have fellowship with him and yet keep on walking in the darkness, we are lying and not practicing the truth. But if we walk in the light as he himself is in the light, we have fellowship with one another **and the blood of Jesus his Son cleanses us from all sin**. If we say we do not bear the guilt of sin, we are deceiving ourselves and **the truth is not in us**. But if we confess our sins, he is faithful and righteous, forgiving us our sins and cleansing us from all unrighteousness. **If we say we have not sinned, we make him a liar and his word is not in us**."
> *(1 John 1:5-10)*

As we continue reading John's full thought, we find that he defines for us what it means to continue walking in darkness. By his definition, to continue walking in darkness, is for a person to say they are without sin and to not be cleansed by the blood of Jesus. Okay. So, just take a minute and think about that. Who is someone who hasn't admitted their sin and been cleansed by Jesus' blood? A Christian? No, it can't be a Christian, because we all know that the one and only requirement for salvation is admitting that you are a sinner and accepting Christ's sacrifice on your behalf.

So, who then? Well, John must be talking about **unbelievers** who reject Christ's sacrifice and their need for it. This also makes 1

John 1:9 (also often misunderstood) make sense as John's solution to the unbeliever's problem, ***"But if we confess our sins, he is faithful and righteous, forgiving us our sins and cleansing us from all unrighteousness."***

In understanding this, we can conclude that the fellowship and confession he refers to in this passage is actually a reference to the relationship and connection we receive at **salvation.** This is an evangelistic passage directed at unbelievers. Therefore, as believers, because we are one with the God of light, we are filled with a light that chases out all darkness and results in being children who walk in the light.

> ***He delivered us from the power of darkness*** *and transferred us to the kingdom of the Son he loves, in whom we have redemption, the forgiveness of sins." (Colossians 1:13-14)*
>
> *"For God, who said, "Let there be light in the darkness,"* ***has made this light shine in our hearts*** *so we could know the glory of God that is seen in the face of Jesus Christ.* ***We now have this light shining in our hearts****, but we ourselves are like fragile clay jars containing this great treasure. This makes it clear that our great power is from God, not from ourselves."*
> *(2 Corinthians 4:6-7 NLT)*
>
> *"For once you were full of darkness,* ***but now you have light from the Lord. So, live as people of light!****" (Ephesians 5:8 NLT)*

Our fellowship cannot be damaged because we can never stop being in full unity with Him.  Our oneness is dependent on Jesus' oneness with the Father.  In order for God to be out of fellowship with us, He would have to be out of fellowship with Christ.  How can we believe that is true?  He cannot deny Himself (2 Timothy 2:13) and so He cannot deny us.  Don't fall for a gospel that isn't good news!

# Holy Nature

RUINING THE RELIGION OF CHRISTIAN SINNERS

As forgiven people who are full of new life that is powered by our oneness with Christ, we have a new nature. This nature has to be in alignment with God's nature because we are one with Him. Scripture calls this new holy nature "righteousness."

> *"God made the one who did not know sin to be sin for us, so that **in him we would become the righteousness of God**." (2 Corinthians 5:21)*

First and foremost, it is important that we take time to understand the word "righteous." Righteousness is one of those big church words that we tend to toss around quite a bit in our religious huddles but don't always take time to think about what it means. The Greek word for righteous is **díkaios,** which, in the simplest sense, can be translated as "innocent, faultless, guiltless, and perfectly right."[6] The ancient Jews would have seen righteousness as something to be gained through keeping and obeying the letter of the Law.

However, when Jesus enters the scene, He teaches us that righteousness is not simply doing righteous things but rather having a heart of righteousness.  In fact, Jesus goes as far as to define righteousness for us as that which is in conformity to God's own being, His perfection (Matt 5:48).  Righteousness doesn't come in stages.  Righteousness is perfection, and unrighteousness is imperfection. With God, being righteous is a lot like being pregnant: you either are or you're not.  There are no degrees or stages of righteousness.  You are either a righteous being or an unrighteous being.  Even under the Law, righteousness was measured by complete and full adherence to all requirements, not just some (Galatians 3:10).  The idea of a progressive righteousness or an ongoing, gradual righteousness is not found in scripture, not even under old covenants.

There is also a clear distinction between how we judge "good" or "bad" and how God judges these things.  God judges with truth, and we judge with subjectivity (Romans 2:2).  We measure our best efforts against others' worst efforts.  God measures us against Himself.  This would be incredibly discouraging for us if our righteous nature was based on our act of doing things right.  How great it is that we have a Savior who lives to be righteousness on our behalf!

---

[6] James Strong, The New Strong's Exhaustive Concordance of the Bible, Nashville: T. Nelson, 1990, s.v. "*díkaios*"

> *"More than that, I now regard all things as liabilities compared to the far greater value of knowing Christ Jesus my Lord, for whom I have suffered the loss of all things—indeed, I regard them as dung—that I may gain Christ and be found in him, not because I have my own righteousness derived from the law, but because **I have the righteousness that comes by way of Christ's faithfulness—a righteousness from God that is in fact based on Christ's faithfulness.**"*
> *(Philippians 3:8-9)*

This passage reminds us that not only have our sins been forgiven, but also we have become the righteousness of God because of the faithfulness of Christ *in* us. This righteousness is not human righteousness but is the righteousness **of God** (2 Corinthians 5:21). So then, it is not just that God sets our past identity as sinners aside, but even more than that, we get credit for Jesus' perfection. This is the great exchange: my death for Christ's life; my law-breaking for His law-keeping; my unrighteousness for His perfect rightness; my old sin nature for His completely holy nature.

*What happens when someone doesn't want to participate in this exchange through faith? How do they get to righteousness?*

Before the new covenant of the cross was the covenant of the Law. If someone were to try to use the Law as a pathway to righteousness, then they would be responsible for perfectly keeping the entirety of the Law on their own (Romans 2:12-13). However, even if, by some miracle, a person was able to do this, still it would not make them righteous but rather it would allow them to be legally declared righteous (justified).

Let's explore this word "justification." It is another one of those common church words that is often left unexplored and unexplained. The word "justification" is most often a legal term. The Greek word for "justified" is **dikaíōsis,** which is the act of pronouncing righteous.[7] You might notice that it is similar to the Greek word for righteous. This is because righteousness is at the root of justification. The word for justification can also be translated as "divine approval." So, if we are "justified" by God then we have been declared righteous and approved by Him.

Obeying God's commandments cannot make a person righteous. The Law can only measure, set a standard, give a list, or reveal what is there (or not there). It is kind of like a flashlight in a darkened room. You can use the flashlight to see the dirt on the floor, but you can't use the flashlight to mop up the mess. The Law is similar in this way. You can use it to see your sin but not to get rid of it (Romans 3:20). This is why sacrifices were required under the Law to cover sin. Only death can deal with sin. Jesus did not **become** righteous because He kept the Law perfectly. He **was** righteous, and the Law revealed that to us.

> **"But now apart from the law the righteousness of God (although it is attested by the law and the prophets) has been disclosed—** namely, the righteousness of God through the faithfulness of Jesus Christ for all who believe. For there is no

---

[7] James Strong, The New Strong's Exhaustive Concordance of the Bible, Nashville: T. Nelson, 1990, s.v. "*dikaíōsis* "

> *distinction, for all have sinned and fall short of the glory of God. But they **are justified freely by his grace** through the redemption that is in Christ Jesus because of Jesus' faithfulness."*
> *(Romans 3:21-24)*

---

Because of our new covenant of grace through Christ, we have been judged by Him and pronounced righteous by divine decree because we have become the righteousness of God. We now have a nature of righteousness. This justification is a free gift of God's favor for us to enjoy! It isn't free because it doesn't cost anything. It's free because Christ already paid the price in full. Grace isn't cheap. It is extravagant and expensive and the cross settled the debt. How could anyone try to offer anything more?

Paul says that those who try to measure and judge righteousness in this way have contempt for the wealth of God's kindness that leads them to repentance (Romans 2:4). The Greek word here for "contempt" is **kataphroneó,** which translates "despise, scorn, and showing it by active insult, disregard."[8] These are people who would actively reject God's free offer of righteousness, disregarding His grace, and turning instead to their own efforts. Paul goes on to say that they are storing up wrath for themselves on the day of judgment, again showing the Christians in Rome, and each of us reading this today, of humanity's total helplessness apart from God's grace. So, really, you are doomed without Christ in you.

---

[8] James Strong, The New Strong's Exhaustive Concordance of the Bible, Nashville: T. Nelson, 1990, s.v. "*kataphroneó*"

God's righteous requirement is a high and impossible standard. It is intentionally this way to show us how much we fall short and point us towards our need for a Savior. Jesus plus nothing is the only righteousness equation.

I recognize that the truth about us having a holy nature is a difficult concept to believe because we still live our lives in a fallen world as fragile humans. And so, even with our new righteous nature, we sometimes behave sinfully. It is easy for us, at times, to fall into anchoring our identity on things which supposedly make us favored or fallen. For the Jews in Rome, it was the behavior of circumcision (Romans 3). For me, most of my life, it was any behavior that the church deemed moral. It's tempting to define ourselves based on our behavior, rituals, and traditions (even good ones), but identity and behavior are different, much like a nametag and a tattoo are different.

Have you ever had a cool nickname that you love? What about a derogatory name? Have you ever been called a critical name on the playground by that one kid that was for sure eating raw eggs for breakfast every day? These names, whether good or bad, that other people here in the world give us, are a lot like nametags. You know what I mean? Those classic red and white stickers topped with "Hello my name is…" They are real and they are attached to us, but they are also flimsy and probably by the end of the day (or within an hour if you're me) will probably fall off and get stuck to the bottom of your shoe.

I was born into a system that attempted to define me based on how many good things I did and bad things I avoided. I spent a good chunk of time as a young adult squirming out from under the fist of this system that I thought belonged to God and chasing after every possible form of immediate pleasure that the world had to offer. I didn't much care or consider who I was harming just so long as I left satisfied. I'll spare you the gory details here since chances are high that my mother is reading this right now, but, you know, use your imagination and you're probably right. I have deep regret about some of those more egregious choices and the enemy still attempts to haunt me with shame over them.

Each of these failures became a nametag of identity that was stuck on my chest. I had all kinds of nametags. Addict. Slut. Failure. Lost Cause. Based on my behavior, these were not unwarranted or inaccurate names for people to call me. By calling these nametags flimsy, I by no means mean that they weren't hurtful because they certainly were, but it was in my discovery that they were simply what I was called and not who I was that I found healing. I answered to each of those names for far too long. It was not until I came to understand the extravagance of God's grace and the true desire of my heart for goodness and love that I was able to get free from the nametags tacked on my chest.

A believer's identity is bigger than behavior. When we take in the life of Christ, when we allow His Spirit to invade our hearts, something supernatural happens. As we learned in our chapter about closeness, we are fused with Him as one being and given a new identity (1 Corinthians 6:17). This identity is not just some flimsy nametag that we can take on and off depending on how we behave that day. No. This identity is *tattooed* on our heart for eternity. In Romans 2:29, Paul calls this "circumcision of the heart." (All the men reading this are very thankful that circumcision is not reversible, I'm sure.) Your true identity will never fade. It will never wash off, and it can never be reversed. It is inked in the blood of Christ and your new identity, your new nature, is holy, without blemish, and blameless.

> *"And you were at one time strangers and enemies in your minds as expressed through your evil deeds, but now he has reconciled you by his physical body through death **to present you holy, without blemish, and blameless before him.**"*
> *(Colossians 1:21-22)*

Sin, then, has been chased out by holiness and is no longer native to us. It is something attached to us that comes from outside of us and seeks to define us and trick us into behaving in a way that does not align with our true nature. Think of sin like a parasite, an invading entity that tries to take over our minds, our emotions, and our will. Sin invades us, but it is not us.

If you've ever vacationed in a less developed foreign country, you probably were told very adamantly, "Don't drink the water!" Why? Because there are parasites in it that could cause you to be sick. If you get sick, does that mean that your body is the problem? No. You get sick because you have an intruder called a parasite that is making you sick. In Romans 7, Paul talks about this invading parasite of sin being at war with his heart and mind making him do things he doesn't want to do.

So, what is the solution to the sin problem? Don't drink the water! Live out of your new holy nature and don't allow sin to make you sick. You have been created for goodness; be who you truly are!

> *"For we are his creative work, having been created in Christ Jesus for good works that God prepared beforehand so we can do them." (Ephesians 2:10)*

The even more exciting thing about this new nature is that you have the freedom to just be yourself. You can live authentically, honestly, exactly as you are in every way. You don't have to make yourself smaller, twist or fold yourself into some box that culture has created for you. You can just be you.

I've talked quite a bit throughout this book about growing up in religion. Well, it gets worse, because I was not only a church kid but also a pastor's kid. (I know, right? Pray for me.) My dad was a youth pastor. My grandfather was a pastor. In fact, I come from a long line of pastors that stretch all the way back to Bradley Hays, a circuit riding preacher in the 1800s.

In my family, the men were the ministers and the women, well, the women were soft-spoken and quiet-natured and well-behaved. And then there's me. And me... well, I'm not any of those things. I've never really fit what others communicated to me that a woman "should" look like. My whole life I've just always been a little too wild, a little too loud, a little too strong, and just generally too much. This left me feeling like I didn't really belong, certainly not in church at least.

It wasn't just within religion that I found myself rejected and told I was less than enough. It was pretty much within every aspect of life. Not only was I not one of those soft, quiet women, but I was also not one of those skinny, blonde-haired girls who liked to share makeup tips and wear pretty dresses. Now, don't get me wrong. There's nothing wrong with those things. They just weren't for me.

Because of my differentness, I believed for a long time that I wasn't good enough, that I was broken just because I existed. Grace taught me just how ridiculous that really is. God doesn't want us to be less than what we are. He made us and enjoys us! Where would the world be if we were all the same cookie-cutter humans? There would be no creativity, no art, and no change or breakthroughs. Our unique beauty is significant to this world. It has power in the spaces we occupy.

That power starts in the deep caverns of your own heart. It starts with you when you're alone. It starts with your choice to not just accept yourself as you are but also to celebrate and be proud of everything that makes you uniquely you. For me, the more I embraced my freedom in Christ, the more I was able to joyfully live out my uniqueness. That came out in silly, superficial ways like cutting my hair short and dying it fun colors (currently fire engine red), gauging my ears, getting fun tattoos because life is hard and I deserve stickers, and wearing fun, bold outfits that may or may not contain obnoxiously bright colors or sequins depending on the day.

It also came out in deeper ways like not having to always protect myself all the time and, instead, letting my protectiveness be used to take care of others, being genuinely joyful, not being so self-conscious about my absurdly loud laugh, and being able to truly relax. Oh, also, I can neither confirm nor deny this to be true, but I have been accused of starting a mosh pit during worship at times. I admit nothing.

Of course, there are still days when I retreat into insecurity and hide for the sake of belonging. There are days when I still pretend to be less than I am; less intelligent, less intense, less deep, or less tender. However, it's no longer every day and it's certainly not my norm anymore. And you know what? People are drawn to authenticity. Do you know how many times strangers come up to me and say something to me about my hair or ask me about my tattoos or women say to me some version of, "Oh, I wish I was that brave!" You don't have to be brave. You just have to know you're free. My uniqueness has become an asset to my ministry and an access point to the gospel for other misfits like me.

> *"Each believer has received grace gifts, so use them*
> *to serve one another as faithful stewards of the*
> *many-colored tapestry of God's grace."*
> *(1 Peter 4:10 TPT)*

You are a work of art. God is proud to show you off as His masterpiece. You don't have to be less to be close to Him. It's all of Him and all of you, perfectly united together. Your nature and His nature are compatible. Not only that, but your unique expression benefits the body of Christ! God's grace is varied, and you are one of the best flavors in the variety pack.

## An Opposing Doctrine: Sin Nature

For some of you super elite Bible nerds out there, you have had a pestering doubt in the back of your mind while reading this that has sounded something like this, "But what about in scripture when it says we have a sinful nature?"

That's a fair question because this idea of a "sin nature" is often misunderstood. This misunderstanding is largely due to translation issues in some (now outdated) Bible versions. The term "sinful nature" was used in earlier editions of the NIV to translate the Greek word **sarx,** which literally means "flesh."[9] This bad translation has led to lots of bad doctrine, making many believe that we as Christians have a sinful nature even after salvation. However, so many other scriptures teach repeatedly that believers are new creations, united with Christ, and have a new, righteous nature (2 Corinthians 5:17; Romans 6:6).

The struggle we face as believers is not with a sinful default nature but with this entity called "the flesh." So, what is the flesh? In scripture this word can be used to refer to our actual physical person, our literal squishy, fleshy body, but it is more often used to refer to our independent humanity. Paul teaches us in multiple places that "the flesh" refers to old patterns of thinking and acting independently of Christ. This is connected to our humanity and **influenced** by sin (Galatians 5:19-23; Romans 8:5-8). This is why Paul calls us in Romans 12 to renew our minds! Because the flesh is simply bad belief and bad behavior, renewing our minds to believe the truth about who we are robs the flesh of its power. We need not be victims of our human fragility. We already have all that we need to overcome it! It is as simple as depending on Christ in us.

As Christians, we are no longer slaves to sin but are now ruled by righteousness (Romans 6:18). Romans 8:9 reminds us that "**You, however, are not in the flesh but in the Spirit...**" The flesh is not our true identity; our true identity is found in Christ, and we get to partake in *His* divine nature (2 Peter 1:4).

---

[9] James Strong, The New Strong's Exhaustive Concordance of the Bible, Nashville: T. Nelson, 1990, s.v. "*sarx*"

Our sin no longer defines us. The label of "sinner" is no longer ours to carry. We are now saints. Yes, saints who sometimes fall for the temptation of the flesh and *behave* sinfully, but it is our *behavior* that carries that label *not* our hearts. Sinful behavior does not make you a sinner any more than flapping your arms and clucking makes you a chicken.

*What about Romans 7?*

> *"For we know that the law is spiritual—but I am unspiritual, sold into slavery to sin. For I don't understand what I am doing. For I do not do what I want—instead, I do what I hate. But if I do what I don't want, I agree that the law is good. But now it is no longer me doing it, but sin that lives in me. For I know that nothing good lives in me, that is, in my flesh. For I want to do the good, but I cannot do it. For I do not do the good I want, but I do the very evil I do not want! Now if I do what I do not want, it is no longer me doing it but sin that lives in me."*
> *(Romans 7:14-20)*

I have a couple of friends who believe this section of Romans 7 where Paul talks about the war of doing what he loves/hates is actually Paul's account of his life before his conversion. They give many good reasons and sound arguments as to why they believe this to be true, and they very well may be correct in their interpretation.

My perspective on this passage is a little different because... well, because I live with addiction. This year, I celebrated my 16th sobriety birthday. Alcohol is still a temptation for me. Though it's been over 16 years since alcohol touched my lips, I still struggle against the addiction. It is a truth about my reality in my humanity. Now, I don't mean that I am defined by my alcoholism but rather that my addiction continues to be a part of my experience in *this* life. I have a new heart securely tangled in the heart of Christ, which means that my identity will forever be as a holy and pure daughter of a sin-forgetting Father. Yet, sometimes, on those grey nights when depression is unrelenting and painful memories remain unforgettable, my mouth still waters with the want of whiskey.

So, you see, this passage looks a little different to me. I can't help but imagine an addicted Paul who has spent his life knocking back shots of sacrifice to quiet his covetous cravings or snorting lines of liturgy to feel the highs of hypocrisy. When I read this passage, what I see here is Paul struggling with the reality of being a human with the heart of Christ.

By the way, do you know what triggered this coveting addiction for Paul? Was it scary, "worldly," evil things? Nope! In fact, it was one of the Ten Commandments!

---

*For indeed I would not have known what it means to desire something belonging to someone else if the law had not said, "Do not covet." But sin, seizing the opportunity through the commandment, produced in me all kinds of wrong*

> *desires. For apart from the law, sin is dead.*
> *(Romans 7:7-8)*

I don't think it really matters whether I have it right or my friends do as it pertains to which part of his life Paul is referring to here. Either way, this passage reveals what happens when we try to use the Law, human effort, or religious behavior to control sin. We end up sinning more! We can't effort our way into holiness. It is a gift given to us as part of our unity with Christ.

We are given this beautiful gift of newness. We become different and, yet, our world stays the same. So then, here we are, these holy beings that are left to occupy a space ruled by sin. Whether this is Paul talking about his life before Christ or simply him revealing his struggle to believe in the holy-hearted human, either way this passage is not about sin nature but rather sin invasion. We see this as we keep reading the passage.

> *"So, I find the law that when I want to do good, evil is present with me.* ***For I delight in the law of God in my inner being.*** *But I see a different law* ***in my members*** *waging war against the law of my mind and making me captive to the law of sin that is in my members. Wretched man that I am! Who will rescue me from this body of death? Thanks be to God through Jesus Christ our Lord! So then, I myself serve the law of God with my mind, but* ***with my flesh*** *I serve the law of sin." (Romans 7:21-25)*

Paul delights in God in his inner being and yet the principle of sin wages war in his "members." Don't we also experience this paradox? In much the same way, sin invades our humanity and seeks to infect us. It lies to us and tries to convince us that it didn't invade us at all but rather that it's a part of our identity in an attempt to keep us from kicking it out.

And that... that is the real truth to be found in this passage.

The real truth is that we are not powerless.

The real truth is that we are not slaves of sin.

The real truth, as Paul says, is that we are rescued by a God unaffected by our humanity. Thanks be to God through Jesus Christ our Lord!

And that means that sin doesn't get to boss us around anymore. That means we can fight the invasion, resist the sin parasite, and depend on Christ for our goodness.

# Total Dependence

RUINING THE RELIGION OF OUR EFFORT

*"I'm a strong, independent woman."*

This is one of my favorite phrases to say, usually very dramatically, after having done something silly like carrying all 15 bags of groceries up the 3 flights of stairs to my apartment in one go. I have to laugh now as I recall one such instance not long ago. I had just spent the weekend serving and teaching at a three-day women's retreat. It was the end of the weekend, and everyone was loading up their cars to go home. For all the other women, their husbands had showed up to help them load up their (far too many) bags and belongings. I, however, do not have a husband. That's fine with me; I've become pretty good at taking care of things myself.

I gathered up my things, backpack on my back, duffle bag slung over my shoulder, and in my hands, my giant tub filled with all the things that, of course, were absolutely necessary for the 72 hours I wasn't in the comfort of my own home. I imagine I looked a bit like a fully equipped pack mule as I shuffled out to my Jeep. One of my friends' husbands saw me and started jogging towards me shouting, "Hey, Jess! Need some help?" In spite of the fact that I was sweaty, tired, and had just walked up a hill that seemed totally unnecessarily placed there by the Lord just to mock me, I heard myself respond, "No thanks. I got it!"

*No thanks. I got it?! Really, Jess? Hard-headed as ever (as mules are I suppose).*

Lucky for me, He knew me well enough to roll his eyes and respond, "Okay. Well, I'm gonna help you anyway," as he grabbed the tub out of my hands and walked it the rest of the way to the car.

This isn't just a Jess problem. This is a human problem. We often try to carry the load on our own, muscle through, and refuse help when we need it the most. Independence is the oldest temptation known to man (literally). It promises freedom and self-sufficiency but only delivers exhaustion and loneliness. Independence is ultimately just fearful self-reliance wearing the mask of strength.

---

*"Now the serpent was shrewder than any of the wild animals that the Lord God had made. He said to the woman, "Is it really true that God said, 'You must not eat from any tree of the orchard'?" The woman said to the serpent, "We may eat of the fruit from the trees of the orchard; but concerning*

> *the fruit of the tree that is in the middle of the orchard, God said, 'You must not eat from it, and you must not touch it, or else you will die.'" The serpent said to the woman, "Surely you will not die, for God knows that when you eat from it your eyes will open and you will be like God, knowing good and evil." (Genesis 3:1-5)*

---

If you look at how Satan operated in the garden, it gives some insight into how he likes to work. Eve is in the garden, and the first thing the serpent says is, "Wow, so God told you not to eat from *any* of the trees?!" Of course, Eve corrects him (she is a woman after all) and tells him they can eat of any tree except for that big one in the middle, the tree of the knowledge of good and evil. Here's the part where he gets really tricky! Then he says, "Well, the real reason God told you not to eat that is because He knows that it will make you like Him!" As we all know, that's when Eve takes the bait.

I don't blame her really. Of course she wanted to be like God! Who wouldn't? Satan doesn't tempt her with evil. He tempts her with independent goodness. She walked with God, lived with God, and had full access to God's presence. Any knowledge she needed was simply a question away. Satan's real lie is, "If you can do it on your own, you won't need to depend on God." He is pulling the exact same con on God's people today!

Satan isn't always this overtly evil guy who comes sauntering in to the tune of something in a minor chord exclaiming "I'm the bad guy, boo!" Sometimes he whispers just enough doubt in God's love, just enough worry, that we lose faith long enough to settle for a cheap substitute, which, by the way, he is more than happy to offer cloaked in forged goodness.

The majority of his temptations for us aren't in what we consider to be "worldly" things. When we talk about "the world" in religious spaces, it is almost always translated to be those things which are overtly evil. You know, sex, drugs, and rock and roll. If we translate "worldly" this way, then what happens is we begin to believe that what we perceive to be "good" must be godly. And so, we become obsessed with doing good things and avoiding bad things, thinking that makes us holy. The greatest temptation of evil is not towards wickedness, but rather, that we need to do more things to get more from God, that our behavior determines God's favor. "Want to know that you're good and not evil," the enemy coos, "just study more, pray more, confess more, and work harder. Didn't God say that?" (Satan loves to misquote God.)

This is the urge of independence. Do it all on your own. Control it all on your own. Free yourself. Heal yourself. Perfect yourself. We even teach this in our churches, touting phrases like, "God will never give you more than you can handle." In other words, you can do it, you can handle it, you've got this. The truth is that scripture says the *exact opposite.*

---

> *"For we do not want you to be unaware, brothers and sisters, of our affliction which occurred in Asia, that **we were burdened excessively, beyond our strength,** so that we despaired even of life. Indeed, we had the sentence of death within ourselves **so that we would not trust in ourselves, but in God***

> *who raises the dead, who rescued us from so great a danger of death, and will rescue us—He on whom we have set our hope. And He will yet deliver us." (2 Corinthians 1:8-10 NASB)*

---

In fact, you can't do it, you don't have it handled, and it *is* beyond your strength. The confidence and joy of the gospel is that despite your experience with things that you can't handle, there is nothing that God can't handle and He is in you. That is where you should set your hope.

The nature of this world, of the flesh, is to seek independence which ultimately leads us to relate to ourselves and everyone else with comparison and judgment. Why? Well, it's simple really, because we cannot ever be enough on our own. We will always fall short. Time and time again we will always fall short. When our worth is measured by our effort, there will always be more to do and more to achieve, forever leaving us with the title of "not enough."

The fruit of the knowledge of good and evil is a mindset of measuring, accounting for, and being defined by behavior. Man was never supposed to take in this fruit because we were not designed to be the determiners of what is good and what is evil. That's God's job. When we are focused on measuring behavior, we completely miss out on enjoying the freedom, peace, and rest that we already have. Same old tree, same old fruit.

This is not God's desire or design for us. Instead, He offers us a better way, the way of dependence. He offers us a new tree (the cross) and a new fruit (righteousness).

> *"I am the vine, you are the branches; he who abides in Me and I in him, he bears much fruit, for **apart from Me you can do nothing**." (John 15:5)*

Righteousness is dependent solely on God's action on our behalf. Our only action is in choosing to receive or reject God's action towards us. That's faith. In Romans 4, Paul uses Abraham as an example of that. Abraham's faith in God's action on his behalf is what made him righteous. It was by Abraham's acknowledgement of his dependence that he was declared holy (Romans 4:13-25). All these years later and nothing has changed when it comes to righteousness. We, just as much as Abraham, are dependent beings. Just think for a second about something as simple as breathing.

It's amazing what power there is in a breath. Life itself can hang on the ins and outs of just one breath. In fact, with very little research, one will find that life's origin lies in one breath. One holy breath. One exhale from God and one inhale from man and life exploded into being. One exhale. One inhale. It's all so simple.

Have you ever stopped to think about what breathing really is? I mean, have you ever *really* thought about it? Breathing is about receiving. Breathing is receiving life from outside of yourself. It's about taking in nutrients and energy and expelling all that is not those things. One exhale from God, and one inhale from man.

It's funny to me how I so often think that I am in control. I cling to my independence thinking that makes me strong. Yet, I cannot even take a breath without being dependent on things outside of myself to supply me with life. On trees and plants and molecules of oxygen that I can't even see with my own eyes.

I can't help but liken this physical life to the less tangible reality of spiritual life. Interestingly enough, in the Hebrew language the word for "breath" and the word for "spirit" are actually the same word. It's the word **ruach**[10] and it carries with it the undertone of both life and power.

You have been breathed into with the holy breath of Jesus Himself. You possess in you the very life force of a Savior too powerful to be held by the grave. None of these things are dependent on any work or effort or achievement by you but rather on simply inhaling.

Many will present lists and guidelines and 10-step programs to live a good Christian life, neglecting the fact that we are wholly dependent on the holy breath of God to accomplish any of those things. Or have we forgotten that even in our breathing, we are dependent beings? We are receivers. God is the giver. May we never confuse the two.

One exhale from God. One inhale from man. That's the gospel.

---

[10] James Strong, The New Strong's Exhaustive Concordance of the Bible, Nashville: T. Nelson, 1990, s.v. "*ruach*"

> *But when the kindness of God our Savior and his love for mankind appeared,* **he saved us not by works of righteousness that we have done but on the basis of his mercy**, *through the washing of the new birth and the renewing of the Holy Spirit, whom he poured out on us in full measure through Jesus Christ our Savior. (Titus 3:4-6)*

Look, I get it.  We humans, we want control.  We want to contribute.  We want to bring something to the party.  And so, we are quick to neglect a gospel that isn't in some way dependent on what we have to do.  We want a script to follow and a recipe to go along with.  We want steps and measurements so that we can see how far along we are.  *Enter Law stage left*

The modern church, for the most part, has set aside the ceremonial Mosaic Law, reasoning that was just "for the Jews," and instead has opted for our own makeshift new version.  This includes the Ten Commandments -- of course, got to have those -- mix in a little bit of tithing -- oops better take out Sabbath because that's Jewish only of course.  Hmmm, let's see.  Well, if any of those old commandments are mentioned in the New Testament, then I guess we should probably include those… and… voila! Law 2.0! I think we'll call it "Christianity."

The number of problems with this Law remixing are almost too many to mention, but I'll do my best to tackle a couple.  First of all, you can't slice and dice the Law.  It's an all or nothing covenant.  And guess what?  The cross didn't change that.  Paul even tells us this about covenants in general, **"When a covenant has been** *ratified, even though it is only a human contract, no one can set it aside or add anything to it." (Galatians 3:15)* Christ completed the <u>entire</u> covenant of the Law so that He could institute a New Covenant with us, namely, grace (Hebrews 9:15).

---

*"For all who rely on doing the works of the law are under a curse, because it is written, 'Cursed is everyone who does not keep on doing* **everything** *written in the book of the law.'" (Galatians 3:10)*

*"And I testify again to every man who lets himself be circumcised that he is obligated to obey the* **whole law.***" (Galatians 5:3)*

*"For the one who obeys the whole law but fails in one point has become guilty of* **all of it***"*
*(James 2:10)*

---

Secondly, you are incapable of keeping the 10 Commandments (or 9 if you subtract Sabbath). You can't even keep one. Listen, I know you think you can do it. They are the big "easy" ones, but you can't. That is why Paul specifically calls the 10 Commandments a "ministry of death" (2 Corinthians 3:7; Deuteronomy 4:13). Don't believe me? Okay. Fine. Let's experiment. We will take the one that most Christians would adamantly say they keep without difficulty, Commandment #1.

The first commandment feels like kind of a given: **"You shall have no other gods before me."** I mean, obviously, we're supposed to only believe in the one true God and no other gods. Because this is such an obvious, all-encompassing, basic-Christian-knowledge commandment, often we make the mistake of thinking that we have the ability to keep it. We think to ourselves, *well, I might not keep all the rest of the commandments perfectly but at least I only worship the one true God and that's really the most important thing.* What this belief reveals is a poor understanding of what this commandment really requires of us.

Allow me to pull a sermon-on-the-mount-Jesus moment and reveal its actual height.

What we take this commandment to mean is that we simply aren't allowed to worship false gods or be atheists. Some modern thinkers may even go as far as to say that we break this commandment when we think highly of celebrities or athletes. Still even this modern expansion is a limited understanding of the truly high standard of this commandment.

First, let's explore what a "god" really is. I like Martin Luther's perspective on this one. He writes concerning this commandment, "to have a god is to have something in which the heart entirely trusts."[11] This view of what having a god is brings about the question: Do we at all times trust God to satisfy our every need? And if we cannot answer yes to this question, are we not already failing to meet this standard?

How often do we trust in ourselves to take care of our own needs? We yearn for and grasp at independence. We clamor for credit

---

[11] Martin Luther, *Luther's Large Catechism* ("The Large Catechism – Part I: The Ten Commandments"), §10

and subconsciously cling to self-salvation from the struggle and brokenness of our own lives. We worship our self first and foremost and cry out to God only when the weight becomes too big for us to carry. See, because we really are poor excuses for gods. And so, we have been tricked into believing that this commandment concerns worshiping something or someone else all while we erect temples to our own abilities and call them "spiritual disciplines."

The truth is, left on our own, we all break this commandment every single day. In every moment, no matter how brief, that we doubt God's ability to satisfy our need, every time that we lack faith, we are guilty of breaking this law and in turn (according to the wages of sin) would be deserving of death. Sounds a lot like Paul's comment that "**whatever is not from faith is sin**" (Romans 14:23). This is the purpose of the Law, to dwarf us under the weight of our sin and point towards our need to depend on a Savior.

This is how God designed it. He knew of our inability to keep even this most basic and simple commandment. He knew we would fail miserably at every attempt to save ourselves. He knew and because He knew and because of the extravagance of His grace, He provided for us a substitute. Because He knew we would never be able to measure up to His perfect standard, He sent His Son to do it on our behalf.

There are many instances during Christ's short time on this earth when He kept this commandment perfectly, but I want to look at just one of these instances. Immediately following Jesus' baptism, He is led into the wilderness where He is tempted by the devil.

> *Then Jesus was led by the Spirit into the wilderness to be tempted by the devil. After he fasted forty days and forty nights he was famished. The tempter came and said to him, "If you are the Son of God, command these stones to become bread." But he answered, "It is written, 'Man does not live by bread alone, but by every word that comes from the mouth of God.' (Matthew 4:1-4)*

Here we have Jesus, who is not just hungry but **famished**, starving, in legitimate need of sustenance, and Satan says to Him, "Hey, dude, you're the Son of God. Why don't you just turn these rocks into food, and you won't be hungry anymore?" What he is saying to Jesus is, "You have the ability to fill your own need." And Jesus says, "I don't need just bread." See, Jesus saw that the depth of His hunger was not just limited to his physical desire for food but went further into His desire for fulfillment and eternal satisfaction. Satan, as he always does, offers Jesus a temporary filling for an everlasting need.

Where we perpetually fail when offered the same temptation, Jesus exponentially succeeded on our behalf. Our lives are burdened by the immeasurable amount of need each day brings, the weight of which we try so desperately to carry on our own. Soon, we are inevitably met with the depressing reality that we cannot satisfy ourselves and once aware of this, we become whiny and unhappy gods.

We are in desperate need of something outside of ourselves. This comes as no surprise to God, which is why he provided a solution before the problem itself existed. He did not just provide, but He lavished. He did not just quench the thirst, but He bathed us in His abundance. He did not just keep the Law on our behalf but offered us life in the midst of our death. He is source when we are need.

The bad news is that none of us could earn goodness through this commandment. The good news is that Jesus' goodness kept it on our behalf. The bad news is we are far more dependent than we realized. The good news is that God is eager to provide us with everything that we need. The bad news is we are incapable of living right on our own. The good news is Christ has made us righteous.

Within the safety of our church walls, we have formulated this idea that God is this untouchable, bright, white, and shiny thing that is far above and away from our humanity. God is way up there and we are way down here and Jesus gets us kind of close to up there but it's up to our religion to get us the rest of the way. So, we live our whole lives working desperately to climb up the ladder of spirituality little by little hoping that we at least get further up than the person next to us.

Sure, the nature of God is perfection, but it's also kindness and love and sacrifice and freedom and life. Sure, He's way up there, but He's also closer than the skin on your bones. That's the whole point of Jesus. God knew we couldn't make it to Him on our own and He never expected us to! We retreat into independence, and He initiates relationship. He does this by entering our humanity and taking our place so that we could be freely given all that He has.

The nature of God is relentless, persistent favor that perfects us.

Either we are dependent on God's perfecting of us, or we are independent and offer the poor substitute of our own efforts. You have to rely on God's strength in you and not your own independence. You can't do it by yourself. You can't exert enough effort to make it happen. In fact, your best independent efforts at overcoming will actually end up making you more overwhelmed. Have you ever noticed that things with God always seem super backwards? God says, "Want to live? Die. Want to be strong? Be weak. Want to lead? Serve." Backwards.

Keeping true to form, we will find that the greatest overcoming power is in humility. And humility is not shown by approaching God with fear and a hung head, but with confidence. Confidence in Him. Confidence that says, "I can't do it, but I know you can." Confidence that allows you to rest in the very life of Christ tangled up in you. Humility is choosing to stop doing and to start being. It's about coming to the end of our own efforts, actions, and duties, choosing instead to allow the creative spirit of our renegade Savior run wild and create authentic, sacrificial love at the very core of our beings.

> *"So then, my dear friends, just as you have always obeyed, not only in my presence but even more in my absence, continue working out your salvation with awe and reverence,* **for the one bringing forth in you both the desire and the effort—for the sake of his good pleasure—is God"**
> *(Philippians 2:12-13)*

Ultimately, faith is a trust fall jump off a cliff. If we don't trust God's heart of goodness, that jump is absolutely terrifying. So, we will try to stop the fall. We grasp desperately for something along the side of the cliff to slow our descent into what is unknown. Soon we discover that nothing holds us as we look down to bloody knuckles, burned palms, and dust between our fingers.

We say, "God, look what you did to my hands! I knew I shouldn't have jumped!"

And we forget that we're the ones who tried to stop the fall, because we were afraid of what was at the end of it. Our broken hands are not a result of the jump, but the resistance of it. See when you resist grace, when you live a life refusing it, attempting to be good enough on your own by your own actions, all you will find between your fingers is brokenness. Brokenness, not as a result of God's wrath, but of our fragile efforts towards independence. Our efforts that amount to nothing but emptiness, failure, pain, loneliness, and everything we are trying so desperately to avoid. Our efforts that, at the end of the day, just leave us grasping at dust.

If you are following after Christ with the expectation that He will somehow make your life nice and tidy and controlled because of your great obedience, I've got news for you... it doesn't work that way. Life with God is wild. Oftentimes when we take off after Christ, our lives become messy and chaotic and we think, "Oh, I must have done something wrong. He must not be pleased with me. I must not be living in God's will."

Imagine how the disciples must have felt as students of a rabbi who led them to touch lepers. Followers whose lives were filled with life-threatening storms, starving crowds, dead friends brought to life, and a triumphant entry to Jerusalem on the back of an ass. These same followers experienced the devastation of betraying their friend, the terrifying calling to spread His message, and the unyielding loyalty to it that resulted in lives wrought with persecution and ending in martyrdom. Do those sound like lives lived in comfort and calm?

For some reason we think God should make our lives easier and so we try to tame him. We plan our sermons and lessons and then we try to fit God into them and call them inspired. The devastating wonder of following Jesus is that we are recklessly out of control. It's a terrifying and comforting truth as it relieves us from having to have it all together all the time but also requires us to live lives entrenched in faith. This faith dares us to believe that God is, in fact, as good as He says He is. He is trustworthy, and we can let go of our own power in exchange for the power of Christ in us.

What is at the end of this trust fall with God?

Love. Joy. Contentment. Acceptance. Healing. Righteousness. Peace. Holiness. Adoption. Friendship. Wholeness. Freedom. Kindness. Unbelievable favor. Oneness with the Creator of the universe. Perfection. Forgiveness. Jesus. Every single positive thing you've ever craved from another person, it's there. He has it, and it's yours!

Just jump.

It's that simple and that complex.

Jump first. Fear later. Grace and goodness are at the bottom.

# An Opposing Doctrine: The Surrendered Life

"It's just semantics."

A line uttered to me countless times over the last decade. A favorite response of Christians more committed to learned rhetoric than to clear truth.

It's just semantics. In other words, "We're saying the same thing; you're just being difficult about my word choices."

*Labored sigh*

Maybe I should clarify. Most of these things that have been labeled as "just semantics" aren't little, superficial, subtle synonyms or casual conversation differences. This isn't a disagreement about if a hot dog should be considered a sandwich or if someone using the word "literally" actually means it figuratively. These are significant topics within our Christian doctrine that influence how we view God and how we view ourselves. Topics like the ones we've covered throughout this book. Ones like whether we are really completely forgiven or if our forgiveness is only good until the next time we sin. When God says He's united with us, are we really one or is that just for heaven someday? When Paul says we have become the righteousness of God, did he really mean that, or was he just talking about how God sees us through His "Jesus glasses" that we invented?

To be fair, I *can* get hung up on words. This is because I believe that the words we choose matter. The words we choose, especially in our teaching about the gospel, communicate something important and become the foundation for what we believe about our faith.

Did you know that, technically, "awesome" and "awful" mean the same thing?

**Awful (adj): inspiring awe**

**Awesome (adj): inspiring awe**

Both words technically mean "inspiring awe," but if I walk up to my friend Allen and say, "Hey, Allen, you're looking awful today!" It would certainly mean something different to him than if I said, "Hey, Allen, you're looking awesome today!" But what does it matter? It's just semantics after all…

To Allen it would matter. To the one on the receiving end, words always matter.

This is why I dislike teaching Christians that we need to "surrender to God."

We throw around this word "surrender" a lot in our Christian circles. Surrender to God, surrender your life, have a surrendered heart. We sing proudly "I surrender all" as a favorite song at late night youth camp altar calls.

The words we use matter because they have lasting impact on how we think about and relate to God. Often, we use this word "surrender" as a call to Christians to give up, give in, let go, and stop fighting against the "Lord's will." Even the primary definition of the word reveals its nature as being something that happens between opposing forces.

**Surrender (v): to yield to the power, control, or possession of another upon compulsion or demand[12]**

There is not a single verse in all of the New Testament that calls Christians to surrender to God. Why? Because we are not at war with Him. He is not a hostile army, and He is not fighting against us. Surrender implies we are in opposition, but God is for us, in us, and united to us. We are on the same team.

I'll play along with the "surrendered" word choice for a minute and let's just say that Christians should surrender. You can't get more surrendered than death. You already died and were raised to a new life that is fully entwined in Christ. You have no more surrendering to do. Life in Christ is not about surrender. It is about dependence. So then, it is not about giving up to a God opposed to us, but rather, leaning into the One inside of us.

---

[12] "surrender." *Merriam-Webster.com*. 2011. https://www.merriam-webster.com (11 November 2025)

> *"I have been crucified with Christ, and **it is no longer I who live, but Christ lives in me.** So, the life I now live in the body, I live because of the faithfulness of the Son of God, who loved me and gave himself for me." (Galatians 2:20)*

Should we rely on Him? Yes. Should we depend on Him? Yes. Should we lean into His strength and stop trying to do it all ourselves? Yes. Any of these are better phrases that are more aligned with the truth of what scripture has to say about a Christian's relationship to God.

Paul uses the word "offer" when He writes on this topic, calling the Romans to offer their bodies as *living* sacrifices to God. This word "offer" means to give, present, or bring before. This comes from a place of choice, heartfelt desire, and joy, not from compulsion or demand. Isn't this a much healthier way to refer to our relationship with God as His kids?

> *Therefore, I urge you, brothers and sisters, in view of God's mercy, to offer your bodies as a living sacrifice, holy and pleasing to God—this is your true and proper worship. (Romans 12:1 NIV)*

I remember going to the park when I was about 4 or 5 years old. I loved to climb anything and everything. I longingly looked up at the monkey bars that were far too high for me to reach. I mean, they were probably as high as the Empire State Building, at a minimum. My dad walked over and asked, "Do you want to try those out?" My eyes lit up as I looked up at him and nodded excitedly. He grabbed me and hoisted me over his head so I could grab the bars. I joyfully took hold of one bar after another as Dad kept hold of my waist. "Look, Daddy, I'm doing it! I'm doing it!" A knowing smile spread over his lips, "Yeah, Jess Babe, *you're* doing it!"

There was no surrender needed between me and my dad. He was happy to help me do something that brought me joy as I leaned on his strength to get me from one rung to another. Why would it be any different with us and our Heavenly Father? In every moment, every day, we are dependent on His strength to get us from one breath to another. He is a proud Dad who delights in supporting His kids. We can depend on Him.


"Look, Abba, I'm doing it! I'm doing it!"

# Fresh Fruit

RUINING THE RELIGION OF SIN MANAGEMENT

As part of a teaching I did once, I asked women to write down their number one fear or anxiety on a card and requested that they give them to me. I did this twice with two different groups of over 100 women each. Later, as I read each card given to me and prayed over them, I noticed a common theme. Of the over 200 cards, 87% of them (yes, I did the math) listed some version of, "I don't think I'm good enough." I believe this is something we all struggle with feeling and thinking at times.

We live in a world that measures our worth based on our work. Our efforts, striving, doing, and performance drive our value in a world whose currency is expectation. God's kingdom is different. The currency of the kingdom is grace and its fruit is love. We don't work to get; we receive what Christ did. We belong because Christ pulled us close. We are capable because He lives in us. Life lived out in Christ is confidence in the truth that you are enough because He is enough. You are enough because He has given you all that you need. You are enough because Dad said so.

> *"Now we have such confidence in God through Christ. Not that we are adequate in ourselves to consider anything as if it were coming from ourselves, **but our adequacy is from God, who made us adequate** to be servants of a new covenant not based on the letter but on the Spirit, for the letter kills, but the Spirit gives life."*
> *(2 Corinthians 3:4-6)*

I have not yet met any Christian who would argue with me about Jesus being our salvation or even that we need grace for our salvation. Where the church seems to get hung up is in the everyday life portion of our faith. We teach *unbelievers* that God loves them no matter what, there is no sin too big for God, and that relationship with Jesus is built on believing not earning. We teach *believers* that their fellowship is in jeopardy, forgiveness requires asking for it with each sin, and that their closeness is dependent on how committed they are to doing Christian things. How exactly did the gospel suddenly get worse after you became a Christian? No wonder we are all so anxious about our enoughness!

This is a symptom of a systemic sickness within the Christian church, the origin of which is a bad belief that grace is only about salvation. The enemy knows he cannot eliminate the truth and so instead, he offers us alternative truths. So, if he cannot eliminate the truth about the fullness of grace then he is more than happy to peddle us a lesser grace that is only good for sin forgiveness and has no actual power for our everyday life. We then end up with a belief system that wants Jesus for our salvation but opts instead for religious effort for our everyday moral living.

Have we learned nothing from the Old Testament about how bad humans are at effort? Maybe it's not that. Maybe it's that we believe Jesus is here to help us as long as we are doing our part to try really hard.

As a teenager in Bible class at the small Christian school I attended, I heard this exact message taught. The teacher (who was very proud of his doctorate in Biblical studies) was teaching on Matthew 5. He read through the passage and stopped at various times to teach us all what we *should* be believing about it. Then he got to the end of the passage, verse 48, which reads, **"So then, be perfect as your heavenly Father is perfect."** He even made the effort to go over to Hebrews 7:19 and take it out of context (literally in the middle of the sentence) citing **"for the law made nothing perfect."** His conclusion? We should try to be perfect but never will be. Don't worry, though. We have Jesus to help.

I raised my hand. He let out a sigh and cautiously acknowledged me (I had a reputation for causing problems in this class). "I have a question," I started very pointedly (he immediately regretted calling on me). "You're saying that God wants us to be as perfect as He is?"

"That's what Scripture says." He answered, dryly.

"But also, we can't be perfect?" I shot back.

"No, we never will be in this life, but that's why we have Jesus. We should try our best and Jesus will help us accomplish the rest."

*Jesus will help us accomplish the rest?*

At the time, I didn't know just how off base he was, but I knew that didn't sound like good news to me and it ultimately, for a while, led to me walking away from my faith entirely. Now I'm older and wiser and I can confidently say that if what he taught was true, then Paul definitely got it wrong when he griped at the Galatians!

> *"You foolish Galatians! Who has cast a spell on you? Before your eyes Jesus Christ was vividly portrayed as crucified. The only thing I want to learn from you is this: Did you receive the Spirit by doing the works of the law or by believing what you heard? Are you so foolish?* **Although you began with the Spirit, are you now trying to finish by human effort?**" *(Galatians 3:1-3)*

This over-educated Christian man had, in fact, interpreted the passages to mean the opposite of what both Jesus and the writer of Hebrews intended.

Matthew 5:48 comes at the end of a long teaching that Jesus, a Jewish rabbi, is doing about the Law (as rabbis are known to do). Unlike many other rabbis, He taught the Law as it was intended, as a great and impossible standard, and so within that teaching He says things like, anger is murder; lust is adultery; if anyone asks you to borrow money you have to say yes; if your eye offends you gouge it out; and if your hand is a problem cut it off. Jesus' intention in this teaching is to demonstrate how high the standard is, culminating in, in case anyone still thought they had it all right, be as perfect as God.

This is not a call from Christ to Christians to work harder, manage sin better, or be more committed. In fact, Jesus' whole point is that we cannot. What this passage should do is not incite more effort from us, but rather, drive us to recognize our great need for His effort in us.

The Law is the standard of perfection. Not only is the Law itself perfect, but it also reveals to us what it means to be perfect according to God. Many people today view the Law as a list of things that we should or should not do. When you look at the Law this way, what ends up happening is that you twist, add to, or subtract from the Law to make it easier and more palatable. God's standard of perfection is high and heavy. We instinctively know this is true; but because we don't also know the true power of grace, we do doctrinal gymnastics to try and wiggle out from under its weight. So, we teach passages like Matthew 5 either as Jesus being metaphoric and dramatic to prove a point or as an instruction to try our best and trust Him for the rest. The Pharisees and religious leaders of Jesus' day behaved similarly.

Some churches teach that Jesus had a problem with the religious leaders because of their adherence to Judaism. This is not true. In fact, Jesus was a practicing Jew in every way. Jesus' issue with the Pharisees wasn't their teaching of the Law. Jesus also taught the Law. His issue with them was that they inserted human tradition and regulation into the Law. They became so obsessed with the words, instructions, and checklists of the Law that they disregarded the heart of it. Sound familiar?

The point of the Law was to reveal our inability to keep it and our need for blood sacrifice to make us right with God. So, then a more accurate view of the Law is to see it not as what we should strive to do but as a list of things we will never be able to do.

This is why Jesus makes those statements in Matthew 5, **"You have heard that it was said, 'You shall not commit adultery.' But I tell you that anyone who looks at a woman lustfully has already committed adultery with her in his heart.'"** In this moment He is essentially saying to them, "Oh, you think you're being perfect? Let me tell you what perfection really is." Jesus always has and always will be about people's hearts. This is the reason He was willing to die for our freedom. He knew we'd never be able to gain it on our own and we were never meant to!

We now have a better hope through which we draw near to God. This is evidenced by the Hebrews passage when read in fullness. I mean, come on, just look at it!

> *"On the one hand a **former command is set aside because it is weak and useless**, for the law made nothing perfect. On the other hand a **better hope is introduced, through which we draw near to God.**" (Hebrews 7:18-19)*

The modern church today has sadly fallen victim to the same behavior of the Pharisees. We try desperately to behave perfectly, to know the rules and follow them all, and to make sure everyone else is, too. In our attempts to maintain control of our holiness, we mix a little bit of God's grace with our watered-down version of His Law, and we end up losing the integrity of both resulting in the poor substitute of only our efforts.

> *So, my brothers and sisters, you also died to the law through the body of Christ, so that you could be joined to another, to the one who was raised from the dead, to bear fruit to God. For when we were in the flesh, the sinful desires, aroused by the law, were active in the members of our body to bear fruit for death. But now we have been released from the law, because we have died to what controlled us, so that we may serve in the new life of the Spirit and not under the old written code."*
> *(Romans 7:1-6)*

What Paul communicates here is that the greatest temptation for us as believers is not the innately evil things in this world but rather the seemingly innocuous sins that wrap themselves around that which is good. Our greatest temptation is not to go out and behave badly, but rather to try and behave so well that God might love us more. Which takes greater faith, I wonder, to know exactly how we should behave and try to control that behavior with all our might **_or_** to trust that God is in control of our goodness?

*So, what then? Are you saying that we should just throw away all good behavior and moral standards and go wild with sin?*

> *"But if our unrighteousness demonstrates the righteousness of God, what shall we say? The God who inflicts wrath is not unrighteous, is He? (I am speaking from a human viewpoint.) Far from it! For otherwise, how will God judge the world? But if through my lie the truth of God abounded to His*

> *glory, why am I also still being judged as a sinner? And why not say (just as we are slanderously reported and as some claim that we say), "Let's do evil that good may come of it"? Their condemnation is deserved." (Romans 3:5-8 NASB)*
>
> *"What shall we say then? Are we to continue in sin so that grace may increase?" (Romans 6:1)*
>
> *"What then? Shall we sin because we are not under law but under grace? Absolutely not! (Romans 6:15)*

---

This question is a common one. One that, it seems, has been on the tongues of Christians since the beginning of the church. I can tell you from personal experience it will be the first question asked the moment you begin to talk about radical grace. "Well, if you go around telling people they're completely forgiven and free, they're just going to use it as an excuse to keep on sinning!" It's a well-meaning objection and condemnation of such action is well deserved to say the least! Although, I must ask: Does your religion's regulation of behavior (aka Law living) keep you from sinning? Did your knowledge of the 10 Commandments keep you from being jealous of that new truck your neighbor just bought? Of course not! Why? Because the Law can only expose sin. It cannot prevent it, manage it, or remove it. So then, it seems that legalism doesn't solve the sin problem.

Which brings us back to that troublesome little question, why not just do evil? The answer to the sin problem is the same answer that the cross gave, grace. Grace became flesh and died to handle sin. Grace overcame the feeble walls of a tomb too small to hold it and brought us life. Grace ripped open the frayed veil that kept us separated and brought us close. And grace lives in our hearts teaching us goodness. Grace, not effort, is the author of godliness.

> *"For the **grace** of God has appeared, bringing salvation to all people. **It trains us to reject godless ways** and worldly desires and to live self-controlled, upright, and godly lives in the present age." (Titus 2:11-12)*

Why not do evil? Grace gives us a simple answer.

Because that's not who you are.

Because you, child of God, have a new heart that is tangled in Christ's perfection.

Because you are no longer bound to a life of evil.

Because it is of no benefit to you.

Because why would you ever want to use your freedom to gain bondage?

> *Do you not know that if you present yourselves as obedient slaves, you are slaves of the one you obey, either of sin resulting in death, or obedience resulting in righteousness? But thanks be to God that though you were slaves to sin, **you obeyed from the heart that pattern of teaching you were entrusted to, and having been freed from sin, you became enslaved to righteousness**. I am speaking in human terms because of the weakness*

> *of your flesh. For just as you once presented your members as slaves to impurity and lawlessness leading to more lawlessness,* **so now present your members as slaves to righteousness** *leading to sanctification. For when you were slaves of sin, you were free with regard to righteousness."*
> *(Romans 6:16-20)*

---

A really good reason to leave sin behind is the fact that you're not its slave anymore.  Let's talk a little bit about slavery.  Most of us reading this have no personal experience with slavery, at least, not in the same way that those in Paul's time did.  Slavery in Ancient Rome was about ownership and belonging.  As a slave you were a possession of another person or family and, as such, everything you did was done under that ownership.

With that in mind, let's consider what Paul has to say about sin and righteousness.  He makes clear in this passage that though we were once slaves of sin, we are now slaves of righteousness.  In other words, we once belonged to sin; but we now belong to righteousness.  Sin once owned us, but now holiness owns us.  We were once possessed by the household of sin and everything that we did, we did under that ownership.  We woke up in the morning and brushed our teeth in sin.  We drove to work every day in sin.  We brewed our coffee sinfully.  Everything we did, we did as a servant of sin.

And then righteousness bought us.

So now we have been purchased by the household of holiness, and everything we do is done under that ownership. Would it make any sense for us to try and serve sin while we belong to righteousness? Of course not! Why? Because we get no benefit from it! That's not where we belong! That's what I think Paul is trying to communicate here. You belong to righteousness, so find your purpose in that and avoid the things that are of no benefit to you.

Paul uses a word here that is often misunderstood, the word "sanctification." It is yet another one of those words that we talk about and use within our religious circles but rarely understand the meaning of it. The Greek word is **hagiasmos,** and it means "setting apart or consecration (specifically for holy purposes.)"[13] In other words, to be sanctified is to have a purpose of holiness. Many people make "sanctification" and "righteousness" synonymous terms, and they are not. To be righteous is to have an identity of holiness and to be sanctified is to have a purpose of holiness. So, in essence, Paul is saying here in verse 19 that your identity as a holy being leads you to your purpose of holiness. Sanctification is a lived-out identity.

Living in awareness of who you are will affect what you do. If you believe yourself to be a dirty, rotten sinner, guess what you're going to do? Dirty, rotten sins. Our belief will always affect our behavior. So, if you want to change your behavior, guess what you have to do? You don't have to follow a workbook or a checklist or chart. You have to do one and only one thing... believe the truth about who God is and who you are. Change your belief, and your

---

[13] James Strong, The New Strong's Exhaustive Concordance of the Bible, Nashville: T. Nelson, 1990, s.v. "*hagiasmos*"

behavior will follow.  Believe you are free, and you won't let sin bind you up.  Look intently into the heart of Jesus, and you will find that love overwhelms the places that fear once occupied.  That's the power of faith.

> *"Do not be conformed to this present world, but be transformed by the **renewing of your mind**, so that you may test and approve what is the will of God—what is good and well-pleasing and perfect."*
> *(Romans 12:2)*

We were saved by faith, and we walk by faith. We were saved yesterday by faith.  We enter heaven tomorrow through faith, and we live out goodness today in faith.  We do not walk this world helplessly.  We tread this earth with divinity in our hearts and, therefore, with divine power pumping through our veins.

*Well, if I have the heart of God, why do I seem to always get myself into so much trouble?*

> *"For if someone merely listens to the message and does not live it out, he is like someone who gazes at his own face in a mirror. **He gazes at himself and then goes out and immediately forgets what sort of person he was.**" (James 1:23-24)*

This is the paradox of being both holy and human, of dirt and grace.  Though we have the heart of God, we find ourselves stuck in a world contrary to it.  So, then, we find ourselves walking the way the world walks and talking the way the world talks because that is all we have ever known. It is our forgetfulness of our identity that leads us to behave badly. It is only after our worldly walking is sabotaged by our God-heart that we begin to notice all that world stuff just doesn't fit with who we are now.

I would even dare to say that if you were to stop and rest, if you were to be still and stop trying so hard, you would find that goodness naturally flows out of you. You might even find that, in your resting, it becomes difficult for you to muster up the ability to do all those worldly things with any kind of happiness. If you had to rely on your own willpower to do good, you would be in a constant state of failure. In His great grace, God provides a solution: His Spirit in you that accomplishes good on your behalf.

> *Now the **works of the flesh** are obvious: sexual immorality, impurity, depravity, idolatry, sorcery, hostilities, strife, jealousy, outbursts of anger, selfish rivalries, dissensions, factions, envying, murder, drunkenness, carousing, and similar things. But the **fruit of the Spirit** is love, joy, peace, patience, kindness, goodness, faithfulness, gentleness, and self-control. Against such things there is no law. (Galatians 5:21-23)*

For any of us who have spent a lot of time in or around Christian spaces, we have probably become very accustomed to certain words and language. We have verses memorized and even sing cute little Sunday school songs about them. But I wonder how often do we stop and consider what the author is trying to communicate? For example, after reading this verse, have you ever stopped to ask, what is the difference between a work and a fruit? We see here two contrasts: the works of the flesh and the fruits of the Spirit. Have you considered the difference between a work and a fruit? A "work" is a behavior, usually one you have to really try hard at. A "fruit" is a natural production of a healthy tree. Does an apple tree have to really push hard to make apples pop up on its branches? No. Apples are produced because that's what apple trees do. The same is true for us!

In my own life this has looked like a development and growth of gentleness. I mentioned earlier that for as long as I can remember I have not liked being controlled, and as a child that looked childish in my pushing boundaries and temper tantrums. In youth, this was just a part of my naturally strong-willed personality. As I grew into adulthood, this natural inclination became fortified by my experiences. I experienced some substantial abuse from people who held positions of authority, ones I was taught to trust.

As I experienced this significant harm from a broken world, that dislike of being controlled turned into a desperate and overwhelming fear of being weak. In my mind, gentleness was weakness and weak was the worst thing a person could be. The weak were the ones taken advantage of; the weak were abused; the weak were tossed aside; the weak were… controllable. So, I became hard. Tough. Stubborn. Immovable and unyielding. I refused to be held down or pushed aside. I was terrified of anyone finding out that I had any soft spots, any tender, squishy spaces that could be poked or wounded. And so, any time I perceived anyone getting close to those soft, insecure places, my immediate response was anger and aggression and distance. I mastered the art of a scathing quip and if you thought maybe my bark was bigger than my bite, rest assured that if my words didn't scare you away, my physical strength certainly would do the trick. Let's just say my fight or flight response was heavily weighted towards fight.

The Spirit has been doing a lot of gardening in my soul since then, especially over the last several years. He has been cultivating in me a new harvest of tenacious tenderness. And the more I allow that tenderness to grow and I rest in its fruit, the less I find myself needing to fight. The less I grab for power or control. The less I am stiff-necked and withdrawn in my relationships. The moment I stopped trying to steal strength for myself from other places was the moment that I realized I had an orchard full of trees bearing strength fruit right in the center of my heart. I suppose that's what God meant when He said that His power is made perfect in our weakness. When I rest in this truth, from it comes a new and vibrant desire to love and serve others well.

We do not need religious strictness for our goodness. We have the fruit of the Holy Spirit in us, the natural production of good behavior from our inner being. Why do we trust Satan to produce badness in us but not Christ to produce goodness in us? Is He weaker and less effective than the enemy?

Grace is actively at work in us. It brings forth our love even for unlovable people. It creates patience in us even amid frustrating situations. It sets our hearts at peace despite the chaos of life. Grace is moving and active. It did act; it is acting; and it will continue to act always moving to the rhythms of love that beat from God's heart. The same rhythms beat from yours. In grace, we have everything that we need to live out the goodness that is now native to us.

> *"I can pray this because **his divine power has bestowed on us everything necessary for life and godliness** through the rich knowledge of the one who called us by his own glory and excellence. Through these things he has bestowed on us his precious and most magnificent promises, so that by means of what was promised you may become partakers of the divine nature, after escaping the worldly corruption that is produced by evil desire. For this very reason, make every effort to add to your faith excellence, to excellence, knowledge; to knowledge, self-control; to self-control, perseverance; to perseverance, godliness; to godliness, brotherly affection; to brotherly affection, unselfish love. For if these things are really yours and are continually increasing, they will keep you from becoming ineffective and unproductive in your pursuit of knowing our Lord Jesus Christ more intimately. **But concerning the one who lacks such things—he is blind. That is to say, he is nearsighted, since he has forgotten about the cleansing of his past sins.** Therefore, brothers and sisters, make every effort to be sure of your calling and election. For by doing this you will never stumble into sin."* (2 Peter 1:3-10)

Peter reminds us here that if we fall for the temptation of bad behavior, it is because we are blind to who we are and we have forgotten that we are no longer sinners. His solution? Be sure of your calling and identity. In other words, know who you are in Christ. This will keep you from stumbling into sin and will empower you to live righteously.

A friend of mine who was just beginning her exploration of radical grace asked me once, "What is righteous living?" She wanted to know what every day might look like living out of grace and not religious effort. I answered simply, "lived-out righteousness." The Christian life is simple really. Trust God to take care of yesterday's failure, trust God to take care of eternity's security, and trust God for today's goodness. Live out what He has already placed in you.

No matter what name you give to it, whether it's good behavior, righteous living, or obedience, the fact remains that it is a *result* of our faith, not a *requirement* of it. It comes at the end, not the beginning. And so, our success in living out what is already true about us lies simply is believing what is true.

We must believe in God's nature of **radical favor.**

This nature led Him to die to remove our sins so we could be offered **finished forgiveness**.

The removal of our sins allowed His **new life** to take up residence in us.

His life in us fused us together so that we could have **complete closeness.**

Our oneness with a holy God results in a new **holy nature.**

This new nature allows us to have **total dependence** on Him for all that we need.

When we depend on Him, He will produce **fresh fruit** in us.

This is the uncommon gospel that ruins religion. The greatest news ever spoken. Why would you settle for anything less?

# Final Thoughts

I'd be lying if I said that I've figured it all out. Just because I'm typing away at truth behind this keyboard in no way means that my mind and emotions cease to struggle in understanding it all. I know very little of the vast grace of God, only that it pursued me relentlessly in the midst of my unfixedness to make me new. Therefore, I reason, grace can never be frightened away by the jagged edges of my humanity; instead, it reminds me that I am not defined by them.

We live in a world where people define one another by their behavior. In our work, in our relationships, even in our churches, we measure one another by how many good things we accomplish and bad things we avoid. This leads to a great temptation for us to hide our struggle behind our shame. If I've learned anything at all about God, it's that He doesn't do things the way we, as humans, do things. In His kingdom, things are backwards, topsy-turvy, wibbly-wobbly. Grace is no different and it roots our identity in Christ's work in us rather than our work for Him.

The wonderful thing about grace is that even when I fail to show it, as I so often do, I am not disqualified from receiving it. There is no cut-off, no point of being not enough, and no time of unforgiveness. Even when I betray grace, I am not betrayed by it for at my weakest it is at its strongest and that is what makes it such a beautiful mess, really. God stacked the deck. He rigged the game. In our losing, we win.

This is the paradox of grace.

My many years of grace obsession have continued to teach me that God is the great saboteur. He slips so easily into our world through seemingly unimportant things to sabotage our mundane with His grandeur. So even when we have attempted to so carefully build up brick walls around our hearts, we awake every morning to find them vandalized by the graffiti of His grace.

This grace is so enormous and so edgy that it wraps me in a state of simultaneously loving and hating it at the same time as it scandalizes my perception of justice with its constant unfairness. And I will continue to choose it. Because it chose me.

In my addiction, grace beckoned me. In my failure, grace exalted me. In my messiness, grace embraced me. In my emptiness, grace satisfied me. When I thought I knew it all, grace taught me something new. When I didn't belong, grace made me a home. I am obsessed with grace because I have yet to find anything that is both as addicting and as satisfying. His grace has been, is currently, and will continue to forever be enough for me.

I am ruined by grace.

Grace is a better gospel. It answers every question. It empowers goodness. It brings life and freedom and joy and *actual* good news. How can we settle for Satan's lesser gospel of effort, striving, and earned closeness? Why are we reaching for fruit from a tree of death and not the tree of life?

This book is dripping wet with scripture. It is soaked in study and prayer, and still some will read this and brush it aside as unbiblical or off base. I hope that's not you. I hope that you will dare to believe in a God who is bigger and better than the box religion put Him in. I hope that grace ruins you and you can't unsee it. I hope you find scriptures in your Bible that you're sure weren't there before but now jump off the page and scream grace at you. I hope your religion is demolished and your faith is fortified. I hope grace wins.

# Verse References

**Enter at Your Own Risk**
- Romans 3:24
- Romans 4:5
- Romans 5:15
- Romans 5:20-21
- Romans 6:10
- Romans 6:14
- Romans 8:31
- Romans 8:32
- Romans 8:38-39
- Romans 15:4
- Galatians 3:1-3

**Radical Favor – Ruining the Religion of a Withholding God**
- Psalm 34:18
- Isaiah 64:6
- John 1:14-17
- John 16:33
- Romans 8:38-39
- 2 Corinthians 1:3-4
- 2 Corinthians 9:8
- Ephesians 2:8-9
- 2 Peter 3:9

**Finished Forgiveness – Ruining the Religion of Begging for Forgiveness**
- Leviticus 16
- Matthew 5:17
- John 1:29
- Acts 2:38

- Acts 3:19
- Romans 3:20
- Romans 3:25-26
- Romans 5:8
- Romans 5:20-21
- Romans 6:10
- Romans 6:17-20
- Romans 6:21-23
- 1 Corinthians 6:19
- Colossians 2:13
- Colossians 2:14-15
- Titus 2:11-12
- Hebrews 4:15-16
- Hebrews 8
- Hebrews 9:22
- Hebrews 9:23-26
- Hebrews 10:1
- Hebrews 10:10-12
- Hebrews 10:16-18
- 1 Peter 1:18-19
- 1 John 1:9

---

**New Life – Ruining the Religion of Killing Yourself**
- Genesis 2:17
- Genesis 3:7
- Genesis 3:19
- Genesis 3:21
- Genesis 3:23
- Genesis 3:24
- Matthew 16:24
- Matthew 27:52
- Mark 8:34
- Mark 15:38
- Luke 9:23-24

- Romans 5:12-18
- Romans 8:3-4
- 1 Corinthians 6:17
- 2 Corinthians 5:14-15
- 2 Corinthians 5:17
- Ephesians 1:1-7
- Ephesians 4:22-24
- 1 Peter 2:9
- 2 Peter 1:3

## Complete Closeness – Ruining the Religion of Damaged Connection
- John 1:1-5
- John 17:20-23
- Romans 6:5-7
- 1 Corinthians 1:5-9
- 1 Corinthians 6:19
- 2 Corinthians 4:6-7
- Galatians 4:6
- Ephesians 2:1-6
- Ephesians 5:8
- Ephesians 6:1-4
- Colossians 1:13-14
- Colossians 1:15-20
- Colossians 2:9-10
- Colossians 3:3-4
- 2 Timothy 2:13
- 1 John 1:5-10
- 1 John 4:9-10

## Holy Nature – Ruining the Religion of Christian Sinners
- Matthew 5:48
- Romans 2:2
- Romans 2:4

- Romans 2:12-13
- Romans 2:29
- Romans 3:20
- Romans 3:21-24
- Romans 6:6
- Romans 6:18
- Romans 7
- Romans 8:5-8
- Romans 8:9
- Romans 12:2
- 1 Corinthians 6:17
- 2 Corinthians 5:17
- 2 Corinthians 5:21
- Galatians 3:10
- Galatians 5:19-23
- Ephesians 2:10
- Philippians 3:8-9
- Colossians 1:21-22
- 1 Peter 4:10
- 2 Peter 1:4

## Total Dependence- Ruining the Religion of Our Effort
- Genesis 3:1-5
- Exodus 20:3
- Deuteronomy 4:13
- Matthew 4:1-4
- John 15:5
- Romans 4:13-25
- Romans 12:1
- Romans 14:23
- 2 Corinthians 1:8-10
- 2 Corinthians 3:7
- Galatians 2:20
- Galatians 3:10

- Galatians 5:3
- Philippians 2:12-13
- Titus 3:4-6
- Hebrews 9:15
- James 2:10

**Fresh Fruit- Ruining the Religion of Sin Management**
- Matthew 5:27-28
- Matthew 5:48
- Romans 3:5-8
- Romans 6:1
- Romans 6:15
- Romans 6:16-20
- Romans 7:1-6
- Romans 12:2
- 2 Corinthians 3:4-6
- Galatians 3:1-3
- Galatians 5:21-23
- Titus 2:11-12
- Hebrews 7:18-19
- James 1:23-24
- 2 Peter 1:3-10

Made in the USA
Coppell, TX
24 February 2026

72256441R00083